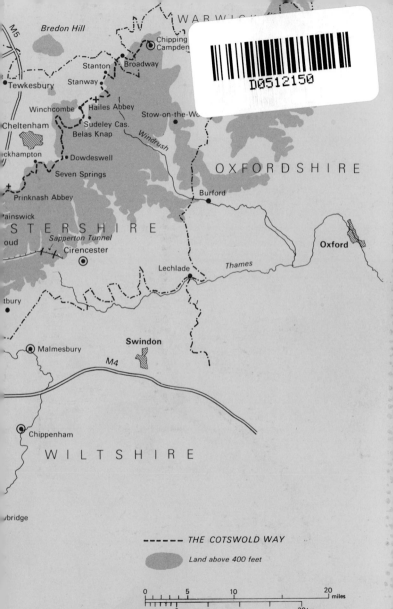

THE COTSWOLD WAY

Land above 400 feet

| 0 | 5 | | 10 | | 20 miles |
| | 6 | | | 30 km | |

A guide to
The Cotswold Way

A guide to
The Cotswold Way

Richard Sale

Constable · London

First published in Great Britain 1980
by Constable and Company Limited
10 Orange Street London WC2H 7EG
Copyright © 1980 by R. G. Sale
Reprinted 1985, 1988
Set in Monophoto Times New Roman 9pt
Printed in Great Britain by
BAS Printers Limited, Over Wallop, Hampshire

British Library cataloguing in publication data
Sale, Richard Geoffrey
A guide to the Cotswold Way
1. Cotswold Way, Eng.
I. Title
914.24′17′04857   DA670.C8/

ISBN 0 09 463210 3

Contents

Contents

Illustrations

The Cotswold Way differs from the majority of long-distance footpaths in Great Britain in not having been designated by Act of Parliament. Routes such as the Pennine Way and Offa's Dyke have been designated under the National Parks and Access to the Countryside Act of 1949 and as such have enjoyed, where necessary, the creation of rights of way where none previously existed. The Cotswold Way travels along currently existing rights of way, although it is possible that an official designation in the future could open up some worthwhile new paths.

The Way owes its existence to the efforts of the Gloucestershire Ramblers Association who submitted a scheme for such a route in the early fifties. The scheme lay dormant until it was taken up by Gloucestershire County Council in the late sixties when the current route, in the main, was designated. Because of the lack of government approval the Way does not qualify for grants to assist in waymarking. Despite this the waymarking is acceptable, the whole route being marked with the symbol of an arrow below a white dot. Occasionally the symbols are sparse, and in such areas care is needed to follow the true line, and so cause no inconvenience.

The Cotswold Way is also unusual among long-distance footpaths in that it travels through a well-populated area, and sometimes seeks towns rather than by-passing them. The walker who has traversed the wilder parts of Britain will find little similarity between them and the Cotswolds, even high Cleeve Hill. But he should not decry the walk for that reason before trying it. In North Wales or Dartmoor the walker, seeking solitude and space, finds man's presence an intrusion. Not so in the Cotswolds. Here man lives with nature, accepting the land for what it is, using the stone from under the soil to build his house and to roof it. Through this use of the local stone a house seems to grow from the land itself, whether it is the grandest of the wool-merchants' houses or the terraced cottage of a weaver.

The route is described from north to south. This is against the prevailing wind direction, but it matters little on this essentially low and sheltered route. Many however may wish to walk the route from south to north to savour the more obviously 'Cotswold' delights last.

There are no real starting and finishing points to the route, except that it runs between Chipping Campden and Bath, but two obvious points suggest themselves – the parish church of St James in Chipping Campden and Bath Abbey.

Though following the escarpment and reaching a height of 1,000 feet the Way is, nevertheless, a lowland route and this, and its closeness at all times to roads and villages, makes it suitable for walkers of all abilities. The walking is enjoyable at any time of year – the woodlands that form a large part of the Way make it especially fine in Spring and Autumn while Summer has warmth and Winter peace.

I would like to thank my wife, son and friends who have contributed to the production of this book by their companionship and enthusiastic support. I am indebted to the library services of Gloucestershire and Avon, particularly to Gloucester City Library for the use of the Gloucester Collection.

Lastly, and most importantly, I would like to thank Mike Rogers for his constant help in all aspects of the production of this guide. Some of the photographs are his work, as is a large part of the technical content of the appendix on Cotswold geology.

Within the guide the route is given in the form of strip maps of approximate scale 2½ inches to 1 mile. Those who wish to see the route relative to a larger section of local countryside should obtain the Ordnance Survey maps listed below.

1:50,000 Maps First Series
151 Stratford-upon-Avon
150 Worcester and The Malverns
163 Cheltenham and Cirencester
162 Gloucester and the Forest of Dean
172 Bristol and Bath

1:25,000 Maps First Series
SP 13 Chipping Campden
SP 03 Stanway, Gloucestershire
SP 02 Winchcombe
SO 92 Cheltenham
SO 91 Birdlip
SO 81 Gloucester
SO 80 Stroud
SO 70 Frampton on Severn
ST 79 Dursley
ST 78 Chipping Sodbury
ST 77 Marshfield, Gloucestershire
ST 76 Bath

Both lists read from north to south. The majority of the second series of 1:25,000 maps are produced as double sheets – thus, for instance, sheet ST 76 is replaced by sheet ST 66/76 also titled 'Bath'.

♠ ♦ ✚	Churches
......·600'······	Contours, 100 foot intervals
♀♀♠♠♀	Woodland
·—·—·—	County boundary
⌐⟍⟋⌐	Field edges and fences
⟋⟍⟋	Streams, rivers and bridges
━ ◣	Buildings
⸝⸜⸝⸜	Cliffs and embankments
◇—◇—◇	Electricity transmission lines
⬭	Long barrows
△	Triangulation stations, spot height in feet
╪╪	Radio and TV masts
┼┼┼┼┼	Railway lines

North is to the top of all strip maps.
Map scale is approximately 1:25,000. Town and building map scales are as indicated on them. Within the text certain abbreviations are used – N, S, E, W north, south, east, west; R right; L left; 12c twelfth century.

All users of the countryside should observe the Country Code which is as follows:

1 Guard against all risks of fire
2 Fasten all gates
3 Keep dogs under proper control
4 Keep to paths across farmland
5 Avoid damaging fences, hedges and walls
6 Leave no litter
7 Safeguard water supplies
8 Protect wild life, wild plants and trees
9 Go carefully on country roads
10 Respect the life of the countryside

Waymarking

The Cotswold Way has been waymarked by the Cotswold Warden Service and the Ramblers' Association using the Countryside Commission's recommended system of painted arrows. Yellow indicates a footpath. Blue denotes a bridleway.

Since this is a national system for all rights of way, a white spot is used to show the through route of the Cotswold Way. In addition on roads a white arrow is used together with the white spot.

The Way is occasionally amended slightly to improve overall continuity.

It is maintained by the Cotswold Warden Service and any difficulties should be communicated to the Head Warden, at Shire Hall, Gloucester.

The traveller who, choosing his day carefully, climbs May Hill, a tree-topped peak at the northern end of the Forest of Dean, is assured of a spectacular view in any direction. But inevitably his eye is drawn eastwards where, rising above the Severn Vale, beyond Gloucester, is what appears to be a range of hills. These are the Cotswolds.

To append the world 'hills' to Cotswold is a misnomer, because in the truest sense there is no range of hills. What is seen from May Hill is the scarp slope of an oolitic limestone mass. The word oolite derives from the Greek 'oion lithos', egg-stone, from the structure of the rock, which is made up of granules resembling herring-roe, about 14,000 to the cubic inch. The geology of the area is dealt with specifically in an Appendix, but briefly the scarp slope runs from Chipping Campden in the north to Bath in the south. In the northern and middle sections, the slope is both steep and high, but in the south it becomes shallower and lower. Behind the scarp, the dip slope falls away very gently eastward to the Upper Thames Valley. There is a pattern of upland and downland superimposed on the scarp-dip geography, but it is marginal. The greatest elevation is reached at Cleeve Hill, a little over 1,000 ft, but there are other points on the 900- and 1,000-ft contours and large stretches of land above the 600–700-ft lines. The illusion of true hill country is given rather by the valleys of the streams draining from the high land down into the Severn, an illusion heightened by their rich, wooded appearance, in contrast to the somewhat bleaker higher land.

Around 1,500 years ago a man named Cod, pronounced 'code', established a farm high up on the tops near the source of the Windrush, near Winchcombe, and in time the place became known as Cod's Wold, Cod's high land. Not only the land bore his name; local villages also reflected his importance in this area: Codswell, Codestan (now Cutsdean) and Naunton Cotswold (which has now dropped the second part of its name).

The name 'Cotswold' was originally used only for that area near the source of the Windrush. Gradually it came to encompass more and more of the Wolds. By 1791 we hear that Bisley, a little north of Stroud, was 'the last parish of that division of the county (of Gloucestershire) called Cotswold'. Eventually the name was used to describe all the scarp-top land from Chipping Campden to Wotton-under-Edge, where the Southwolds took over. However, since there is no break in the geology, and only a slight, but significant, change in scenery, the Cotswolds are now taken as the name for all the uplands as far south as the Avon Valley at Bath.

The history of the area starts far earlier than Cod. The last Ice Age, some 25,000 years ago, did not reach the Cotswolds, but the melt-water widened the Severn, creating, in the area between the river and the base of the scarp, a densely vegetated, waterlogged semi-marsh. With the end of the Ice Age the first inhabitants also arrived. They were hunters of the Mesolithic, or Middle Stone Age, who trailed the herds in the forests of the scarp top in preference to seeking a living in the inhospitable river valley. They have left few traces of their passage, the nomadic existence being unsuited to the collection of many possessions. What they have left, flint hand-axes and scrapers, points to a precarious existence. The Cotswold forests were full of game animals but were also dangerous, inhabited by wolves and wild boar.

The post-glacial forest at first comprised pine and birch, but this was gradually replaced, as the climate changed, by oak and elm, and then by beech, the characteristic woods of the Cotswolds as we see them today. In parallel with this change, the woodland man was also changing, clearing the forest to make it less dangerous and to enable him to provide grazing and protection for the half-wild pigs and cattle he now possessed. By the Neolithic or New Stone Age, the area had assumed some importance. The Neolithic people were farmers rather than hunters, and found in the high Wolds what they needed, large areas of reasonably fertile soil, with beechwoods to provide beechmast for their pigs. The stationary life-style that these factors helped to produce also gave rise to the oldest permanent monuments to man's existence in the area, the long barrows. There are about a hundred of these, and their design is so specific that they have been given a class name of their own – the Severn-Cotswold type. The barrow was, essentially, the burial

mound of the tribal chieftains and their families, and points to the
power that the chief had over the local people. A large barrow might
contain 5,000 tons of stone, some of it in the form of large, shaped
slabs, and its construction could take many thousands of man-
hours. Such a work required not only a secure leadership, and
excellent man-management, but also a well ordered life-style that
allowed men to be freed from food production for considerable
periods.

The barrow was built up around tombs of upright and roofing
slabs surrounded by a dry-stone retaining wall. The whole was then
covered with turf, the slippage of which forms the grassy ovals we
see today. At the entrance, which was invariably at the east end,
there were horns of dry-stone wall curving inwards around the stone
portal. Later, for reasons not well understood, the portal became a
false entrance, the true burial chambers being placed along the
length of the barrow. The horns were obviously significant, and it
has been suggested that the people worshipped the Earth Mother,
interment being seen as a return to the womb, as was the setting of
the sun each evening. This would also explain the east-west barrow
orientation and the foetal burial position. Often the dead person was
buried with weapons, tools and pots containing food and drink.
Some tombs contain small collections of shells, and others of
especially smooth, coloured stones. In their original form, the
barrows must have been spectacular objects, sited so as to be visible
over the greatest possible distance. The Cotswold Way passes two of
the finest barrows: Belas Knap, a false-portal type, and Hetty
Pegler's Tump, a true-entrance type.

The barrow-builders dominated the area for around a thousand
years, and were replaced eventually by the early Bronze Age people
– the Beaker folk, famous for their association with Stonehenge. The
Beaker people did not wipe out the Neolithics, the process being one
of gradual absorption with intermarriage, but eventually the culture
of the area changed. The most obvious sign of the change is that
individual interment following cremation replaced communal burial.
The form of the burial mound also changed, the round barrow
replacing the long barrow. There are some 350 round barrows in the
area. None of any importance lies on the route but they are, in any

case, small and rather insignificant mounds. The word 'Beaker' in the name of these Bronze-Age people derives from their habit of including in the burial-mound a beaker of specific design.

The Bronze Age lasted, in its turn, a thousand years before the area was submerged in the flood of Iron-Age immigrants from continental Europe. The Cotswolds became the home of a Belgic tribe called the Dobunni, and it is to them, primarily, that we owe a second notable feature of both the area and the Way – the hill fort. Originally the forts may have been little more than refuges for the local dwellers when danger threatened, but later, as the excavations of the Crickley Hill site, on the route, have shown, they were larger and more impressive structures containing a village of long-houses. What we see as ramparts today are usually only the grassed-over rubble bases of stone walls that were topped with defended wooden walls, while the ditches have been filled by creepage. Later forts had a succession of ramparts and ditches, probably arising from the advent of the sling as a weapon of war. The Dobunni were civilised people living in houses with laid floors, having doors with latches. The women wore jewellery, the enamelled and engraved bronze mirror found in a lady's grave at Birdlip being, arguably, the finest piece of Iron-Age craftsmanship so far discovered in Britain. Civilised or not, however, the Dobunni were under almost constant threat of annihilation from the Silures in Wales and other Belgic tribes to the south and west. In the circumstances it is hardly surprising that when the Romans invaded Britain in AD 43 the tribe offered no resistance, appearing to have treated them as liberators. There was a token show of resistance at the hill fort at Minchinhampton, not by the Dobunni but by remnants of Belgic forces retreating before the Romans. The Romans destroyed the fort and secured the area, making a camp at Gloucester where the Severn could be crossed easily. This camp served two purposes: first as a base for action against the Silures, and secondly to prevent incursions into the area by them. The Silures were obviously a source of considerable concern, a full legion being brought from Colchester to assist in the operations.

As usual, the Romans made a significant impact on the area, and nowhere is this more evident than at Bath, which lies at the southern

end of the route. There are also well-preserved remains elsewhere
that rival any in Britain: the villa at Chedworth and the mosaic floor
of the huge Woodchester villa. Neither of these sites is on the Way,
but the route passes close to the smaller villas of Wadfield and
Witcombe, each of which gives some idea of the luxurious life style
of the wealthier Romans, and the care with which they chose their
sites to provide a sunny aspect and running water. During the long
centuries of Roman occupation, life in the Cotswolds seemed secure
and well-established, until the withdrawal of the legions in AD 410
made it impossible to resist the incursions of the Saxon invaders.
Little is clearly known of the Dark Ages that followed, when the
legend of King Arthur, defender of the realm of Britain, arose.
Some reports speak of a battle in AD 577, in which the British were
decisively beaten at Dyrham, an unmarked battlefield that lies on
the Way. The area became the domain of the Hwicce Saxons,
though existence for the settlers was not, for a long time, peaceful.
According to tradition, the Hwicce were West Saxons who held
allegiance to the kings of Wessex, but they also shared a long border
with the kingdom of the Mercian Saxons to the north. They and
their lands were consistently troubled by the power struggle between
the two rival kingdoms. Periods of relative stability did occur,
however, and during one of these a monastery was founded at the
Mercian capital of Winchcombe, on the Way, and another to the
south at Bath.

Eventually, when the country was united under one king,
Gloucester emerged as an important centre, standing as it did at
the head of the Severn and on the Mercia-Wessex border, with the
Cotswolds forming a defensible high-level route between North and
South England. Edward the Confessor came there in the first year of
his reign to hold his Witan with the three great Saxon Earls,
Godwin of Wessex, Leofric of Mercia, and Siward of Northumbria.
Following this, he came there each winter during his reign, a
practice that continued in the reigns of the Norman kings after the
conquest of 1066.

The Normans have made a lasting impression on the area in the
form of the string of fine churches in the villages that straddle the
ridge. Though some have been reconstructed and others, sadly,

mutilated by the Victorian restorers, they stand as a monument to the Norman age.

Under Norman rule, the area maintained its importance, and Gloucester at one time became the capital of England, though only briefly, during the civil war between Stephen and Matilda. When Henry II came to the throne, he granted Gloucester its first charter as a city. The area grew rapidly in economic wealth under later kings, its rise in fortunes being due in large measure to the Cotswold sheep.

The sheep, known as Cotswold Lions, fared well on the grass of the high Wolds. There was also an abundance of water-power in the streams draining down to the Severn Vale, and deep layers of fuller's earth. These made the area the centre of the English clothing trade. At first the local industry had been the production of raw wool, but a clothing industry grew up using craftsmen from the Low Countries. In the mid-14c, England exported about 4,500 cloths per annum. Two hundred years later it was over 120,000 per annum. England's prosperity depended to an enormous extent on the trade, and more than half the exports were manufactured in the Cotswold area. It is estimated that at its height the Cotswolds held half a million sheep, and that the trade employed half of all the area's workers. The importance of the trade can be seen in the way it has passed into our folklore. The Lord Chancellor sits on a woolsack, a memorial to the industry, and we still use, though perhaps not for much longer, the 14-lb stone weight. The 'stone' was held by the farmer, an actual stone that was tested against true weights carried by the buyers. When found to be accurate, the two weights were used to weigh out the fleeces, a good fleece weighing 28 lbs, or 2 stones. The industry around Stroud produced a particularly fine scarlet cloth, so distinctive that it was selected for the British army, Cotswold scarlet being the red of the thin red line.

The wool trade created the Cotswolds as we see them today. Many of the towns contain houses erected by the rich wool merchants of the day, notably Chipping Campden and Painswick, both on the Way. The merchants were also great benefactors of the Church, in some instances giving money for the building of magnificent new churches, the Wool Churches, several of which are also on the Way. In them are memorials to the merchants, treasures of brass and alabaster. A particularly fine example of a Wool Church starts the Way at Chipping Campden.

The prosperity was interrupted, in brief but bloody fashion, by the Civil War. Evidence of the war can still be seen in the area. The Way passes a stone commemorating the raising of the siege of Gloucester in 1643, and the church at Painswick still bears signs of a short but deadly skirmish fought between bands of rival soldiers.

After the Civil War, however, the wool industry went into a general decline. In an effort to halt the decline, the government tried different ideas, the most obviously desperate being the 'Burial in Woollen' Act, which stated: 'from and after 1st August 1678 . . . no corps of any person . . . to be buried in any stuffe or things other than what is made of sheep's wool only'. This and other measures were ineffective and the decline accelerated in the 18c. The change was felt most severely by the workers in the industry – the parters and brayers, the shearmen, spinners and weavers. The mill-owners cut wages to maintain profits, and riots followed, the suppression of which was both inevitable and disastrous for the rioters. Whole families starved or moved from the area. Efforts to revive the area's fortunes by the building of the Stroudwater Canal, crossed by the Way, and the construction of new, up-to-date mills with new machinery, as at Kings Stanley, also on the Way, were tried. Though they stemmed the tide briefly, it was all to no avail and the industry died. Towns in the south – Dursley and Wotton – survived through being large enough and close to Bristol, but for the rest the fall was absolute. It is a strange quirk of fate that the decline that cost the workers so dear has allowed the Cotswold villages to maintain their original character, and so endeared the area to tourists.

After the decline of the wool industry, the northern Cotswolds returned to an agriculturally based economy, while the southern Cotswolds became more industrialised, with an economy based on Bristol. The Severn Vale itself saw two examples of that most modern of structures, the nuclear power station, constructed at Berkeley and Oldbury-on-Severn and, from the latter, the elegant bridge that now spans the river can be seen.

1 The High Wolds

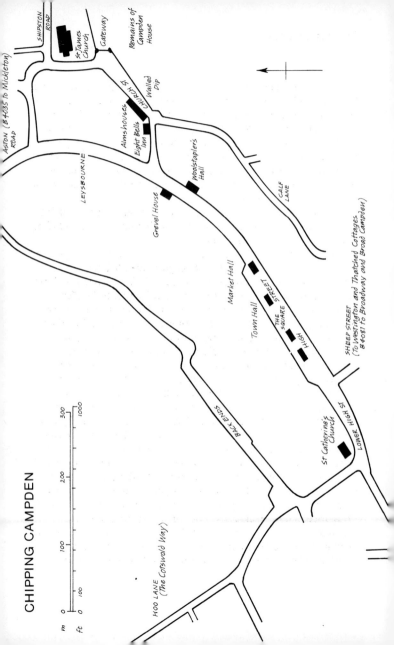

CHIPPING CAMPDEN

The name Campden derives from the Saxon 'camp-denu', meaning a valley with enclosures, to which was added the standard form 'ceping', a market. This latter word appears frequently in English place-names (Chipping Norton, Chipping Sodbury) and is also the root of Cheapside in London. The first Saxon settlers found good land here, and they were also close to one of the salt ways coming south from Droitwich. Salt was important at the time because the scarcity of winter fodder necessitated the killing off of animals which were salted down for the winter.

By the time of Domesday, the manor of Campden had about 300 inhabitants and was held by Hugh, Earl of Chester. That population compares with about 2,000 today.

Campden also saw one of the more curious miscarriages of justice that have occurred in Britain. On 16 August 1660, William Harrison, a gentleman, and steward to Lady Juliana Noel, the eldest daughter of Sir Baptist Hicks, went out to collect rents for Her Ladyship as he had done previously; he had been a faithful servant of the family for 50 years, and at the time he was nearing 70. When he did not return at his usual time, his wife sent John Perry, his servant, to look for him. Perry did not return either. The next morning Harrison's son Edward, leaving home to search, met John Perry returning to the house. Perry had an odd tale to tell; he had met various friends with whom he had talked, had been afraid to continue because of the dark, and had slept for an hour in a hen-roost. Then, overcoming his fear, he had continued the search, only to become lost in the mist so that he had to wait the night out under a hedge. Edward Harrison and Perry continued the search together, and met an old woman who showed them a blood-stained comb and hat-band she had found. The men immediately identified them as Harrison's and a full-scale search was organised, but no other sign of Harrison was found. Suspicion fell on John Perry, whose story of meeting friends was checked and confirmed. Nevertheless he was detained and questioned, and during the questioning his story began to change, eventually becoming quite bizarre. First he said that a wandering tinker had waylaid Harrison, then that a gentleman's servant had killed him, and then that he had been murdered and thrown in a rick of beans. The rick was searched without success. Finally, to everyone's astonishment, Perry said that his mother, Joan, and brother, Richard, had killed Harrison after robbing him. Later he admitted that he had been present when Richard strangled Harrison and had helped him to throw the body into a nearby mill-pond.

Joan and Richard were arrested, both protesting their innocence, and the pond was searched for the body. No body was found. John Perry now said that his mother and brother had, the previous year, robbed Harrison of £140. This, too, they denied, but at their trial in the autumn of 1660 they pleaded guilty to it so as to gain the benefit of the recent Act of Idemnity. In the absence of a body, the judge declined to try any of the three for murder, but they were not re-leased. In the spring of 1661 they were brought before a more amen-able judge and all three were found guilty and sentenced to death.

Lady Noel used her influence to have the executions carried out on Broadway Hill as an example to the local people. As was usual at that time, crowds turned up for the event. Since there was a local belief that Joan Perry was a witch and had bewitched her sons, it was decided to hang her first to break the spell. Next was Richard, who implored John to tell the crowd of his innocence and save him. His pleas were to no avail and John watched apparently unmoved as his brother died. Only then did he start to protest his own innocence, saying that the story was not yet over and that one day the crowd would know the truth. Following the executions, Joan and Richard Perry were buried beneath the gallows, while John's body was hung in chains to rot.

Two years later William Harrison walked into his home. He claimed that, while out collecting rents, he had been attacked by three men, knocked down, tied up, robbed, and thrown into a pit. Later he was taken to Deal and put on to a ship, which after six weeks' voyage was attacked by two Turkish warships. Harrison was taken prisoner and sold as a slave in Smyrna, but escaped and made his way on foot, through many perils, across Europe to Lisbon. There an unknown man paid his passage to London, and he had walked thence to Campden.

This story is improbable, and in a careful assessment of the evidence in 1959 by Sir George Clark, it is suggested that Harrison had been embezzling money from the Noels for some time during the frenzied years of the Interregnum and was afraid that the return of the rule of law would uncover the deed. He therefore contrived, with Perry's help, to fake a robbery and disappear for two years, during which time he lived on the embezzled funds. An alternative story was that he was spirited away by the Noel family itself so that his knowledge of their supposed anti-Royalist behaviour would not cause embarrassment. Of the two, the former is the more likely, though it implies that Harrison allowed three people to die for a crime he knew they had not committed. It is apparently true that following his return his wife hanged herself. Harrison himself continued in the Noel employ until he died at the age of about eighty.

Our route starts, officially, in the High Street, but if we regard the church as the starting-point, the Way not only takes in the best of Campden but also starts and ends at monuments to the Cotsaller's skill with stone – from Chipping Campden Church to Bath Abbey.

The church is reached after a short walk through an avenue of twelve lime trees, planted in 1770 in honour of the twelve apostles. The church itself is a fine example of a Cotswold Wool Church, built in the 15c by the town's newly rich merchants. It was not entirely new, since it occupied the site of previous churches and incorporated some parts of the older buildings, parts of the S wall dating from the mid-13c. The 15c building which we see now was constructed in the Perpendicular style following a bequest by William Grevel, who is commemorated inside. Being of a single style, it has a certain completeness, and the elegance of line is enhanced by the tower, which is, arguably, the finest of any Cotswold church besides being one of the tallest. The tower – notice the twelve pinnacles on top – is reputed to have been built by John Bower, who was also responsible for the Lady Chapel in Gloucester Cathedral.

The church is entered via a porch which has several scratch dials (incised sundials). If the outside is a masterpiece of elegance, the inside is a treasure-house of the unusual, if not always the artistic. If you turn L on entering the S aisle, the door beyond the font leads to the muniment room, which was once used as a school-room. It now houses an exhibition of old church records, and also the only surviving relic of the first Norman church, the corbel (roof timber support) depicting a muzzled bear. Continuing along the back (W) wall of the church, the tower is reached. It contains two of the finest pieces in the building, the first being a cope of the late 14c. It is of crimson velvet, nearly 11 ft along the edge, with a 2-in. blue border, edged with yellow and worked with gold roses. It is still possible to make out the figures of saints, although they are damaged, and the groundwork has completely disappeared. The cope was restored by the Victoria and Albert Museum and is one of the few from the time of Richard ii still in existence. The second piece is a perfect set of altar cloths of the 15c. The cloths were probably given to the church in 1488 by William Bradway and are unique as a perfect set. The material is rich white silk damask, and the embroidery includes a superb representation of the Assumption. The set was copied by the command of Queen Mary for the High Altar of Westminster Abbey for the coronation of King George v and Queen Mary on 22 June 1911.

Continuing now down the nave, to the R is a fine Jacobean pulpit presented to the church by Sir Baptist Hicks in 1612, and to the L an equally fine brass falcon lectern given by him in 1618. The brass falcon is of Flemish origin and was bought for £26. The pulpit is richly carved and inscribed 'Ex Dono Benigni Baptistae Hickes'. Near it stands half of the old Norman font. This beautiful structure was mutilated in 1727 by one Rowland Smith to make way for a pew for his tenants. The deed did not pass without comment; the ripples had not died down by 1737 and assisted in saving the Thomas Smith monument which the vicar wanted to remove in order to clean up the chancel.

This is a striking feature of the chancel, a canopied tomb on the N wall. Smith was a lord of the manor who died in 1593, having spent much time at Henry viii's court. The full-length effigy of Smith, in armour, is surrounded by the kneeling figures of his two wives and thirteen children. The chancel is also rich in brasses. The oldest of

Chipping Campden: The tower of St James' Church beyond the 17c almshouses

these is the Grevel brass, commemorating William Grevel (d. 1401)
and his wife. Grevel was the local merchant previously mentioned
for his contribution to the building of the church. His other bequests
include the Richard II cope. Such bequests were not unusual
amongst the rich merchants of the day. The brass is the largest in
Gloucestershire, and one of the oldest. The inscription, translated,
reads:

'Here lies William Grevel of Campden, formerly a citizen of
London and the flower of wool merchants of all England, who
died on the first day of October Anno Domini 1401.'

It is probable that Grevel built his house in High Street for his use
late in life. In the brass he is depicted with the short hair and forked

beard that characterised the merchants of the day. His wife's dress is also worthy of note, being fastened with more than 80 buttons.

In addition to the Grevel brass are those of Welley, Lethenard and Gybbys, dating from 1450, 1467, and 1484 respectively.

From the chancel continue to the South Chapel, which was given to the church in the early 1600s to house the remains of the Hicks family and their successors. This Chapel may be seen either as a treasury of fine, monumental masonry, or as a demonstration of an overwhelming self-indulgence. Holding the centre of the stage is the canopied tomb of Sir Baptist Hicks, first Viscount Campden, and his wife Elizabeth. The couple are depicted in full-size alabaster effigies representing them in their coronation robes. The effigies are of considerable craftsmanship, as are those of Sir Edward Noel and his wife Juliana, the eldest daughter of Sir Baptist and Lady Hicks, on the S wall. It has been maintained that they represent the finest work of Joshua Marshall, Master Mason to Charles II. It may be thought, however, that the larger than life-size figures dressed in shrouds in the act of resurrection on Judgement Day are a little bizarre. Lady Juliana Noel had the sculpture erected in 1664 in her own lifetime, after the death of Sir Edward in 1642. The doors of the tomb were kept closed until her own death, when they were finally opened to reveal the reunited couple hand-in-hand. The doors of the tomb are inscribed with brief biographical notes. Those of Sir Edward quote his titles, 'Viscount Campden, Baron Noel of Ridlington, and Hicks of Ilmington', and refer to his death 'at Oxford at ye beginning of the late Civil wars, wither he went to serve and assist his soverain Prince, Charles the first'. Lady Juliana is described as 'a lady of extraordinary great endowments, both of virtue and fortune'. One of her children, Henry, will be met again later in the route, and another, Penelope, is the subject of the beautiful monument on the chapel's E wall. Penelope died unmarried in 1633, aged 22, having contracted blood poisoning after pricking her finger while embroidering. The marble bust is thought to be the work of the Italian sculptor Francesco Fanelli. The inscription speaks of her 'pretious Dust here preserved' over which her 'sad Parents . . . dropt their Teares and Erected this Marble to the Deare Memorie of their . . . losse'.

The door is reached again by passing down the S aisle. In the Middle Ages this was a chantry of St Katherine. Tradition has it that there was an earlier chapel to St Katherine in Campden built in the late 12c by Hugh de Gondeville, who held the manor from 1173. He was the leader of the knights who in 1170 murdered Thomas à Becket. He is said to have built the chapel, possibly sited where the Town Hall now stands, as an act of penance for the guilt he felt in later life.

The churchyard is tidy but undistinguished. It offers an interesting prospect, however, if the newer extension to the S is visited. From here can be seen a pavilion that is all that remains of Campden House, built by Sir Baptist Hicks and completed around 1615. Sir Baptist himself arrived on the Campden scene in 1606 when he bought the manor. He was a mercer (a dealer in textiles) and financier from London, with Gloucestershire antecedents. He was incredibly rich even by the standards of the day and had been made Contractor for the Crown Lands by James i who borrowed immense sums from him on various occasions. He lived in London, having built the first country house in the village of Kensington on land he won at cards. This house was named after Campden and stood on the site of the present Campden Hill Square. Soon after obtaining the manor, he decided to build himself a country seat in Campden, which he did at a cost of £29,000, with internal decorations costing an extra £15,000. The market hall, which he bequeathed to the town, was built at a cost of £90. The house, which not surprisingly upset many of the locals at the time by its ostentatious splendour, was of local stone in an ornate Italian style, with water- and terraced gardens and banqueting halls. It also had a transparent roof-dome which was lit up at night to assist late travellers to Campden. The interior of the house was finely decorated with marbles and plaster and contained many expensive works of art. Of the house, only drawings and the banqueting halls still exist. The halls closed the ends of a great terrace and had basement rooms opening on to the gardens. The curious twisted spiral chimneys of the halls were a feature of the house as well. The house and gardens, which covered 11 acres, were taken over by the Royalist forces in the Civil War and, on 7 May 1645, the main house was razed by fire following the withdrawal of the garrison for the defence of Evesham. Why exactly the house was burnt is a matter of dispute. The official reason given at the time was to prevent it from becoming a garrison for Parliament troops, but other Royalist sources referred to the burning later as an act of barbarism. It is possible that the fire was an accident, following a final drunken brawl of the troops, or perhaps an act of rebellion on their part following the cutting short of their quiet life for the greater risks of actual combat.

The only other remnant of the great house is the arched gateway, which stands next to the entrance to the church. It is flanked by a pair of lodges, with solid stone roofs and chimneys which form the pediments of the gateway.

Leaving the church and gateway, the route goes down Church Street. To the R are the almshouses built by Sir Baptist Hicks in 1612, at a cost of £1,000, to house 12 poor people – 6 of each sex.

Chipping Campden: The gateway, beside the church, that is all that remains of the Hicks' mansion

The houses were built in the shape of an I, probably as a mark of respect for James I, Hicks's employer. With the raised pavement which sets them off, and their elegant tall chimneys, the houses are one of the most photographed features in Campden.

Opposite them in an interesting relic of a former way of life – a walled dip which was once filled with water and used to soak the wooden wheels of carts to prevent them from drying and shrinking. Near the bottom of Church Street is the 14c Eight Bells Inn, used to house the stonemasons who constructed the church. Now turn L into Campden High Street, which is without question the showpiece not only of the town but of the entire area. This magnificently wide curving street, with its houses whose exteriors are alive with ancient character, seems to personify the way in which the Cotswold stonemason has brought together the craft of man and the gifts of nature. Almost every house in the street has some story to tell, but only the more notable can be mentioned here.

First, on the R, is Grevel House, built in 1380 by William Grevel, whose memorial brass has already been seen in the church. The house has changed little since Grevel's day, and still contains his study. The double bay windows are an extremely rare feature, and the sundial and curious gargoyles give it great charm. Opposite Grevel House is Woolstaplers' Hall, the only other intact – though in this case altered – 14c domestic building in Campden. The hall was built at the same time as Grevel's by Robert Calf, whose name is commemorated in Calf Lane at the back end of the building. The name now given to the building derives from its use as a meeting and buying place for the merchants of the wool staple, the staple being the raw fleece. The large hall used by the merchants still exists on the first floor. The building houses a museum of curios acquired by the owners over a number of years. The exhibits have now overflowed into Bedfont House, perhaps the finest of the 18c houses in the High Street, built about 1740 by Thomas Woodward, a mason and builder. Much of the High Street was altered at about this time, but there are two notable exceptions – the town hall and the market hall.

The market hall, built in 1627 by Sir Baptist Hicks in the Jacobean style, was constructed simply as a shelter for the local market, but its gables and arcades suggest the sumptuous style typical of its builder. The nearby town hall is a curiosity. It is certainly true that the panelled buttresses on the S side are of the 14c or earlier, but the theory that they represent the last remnants of Hugh de Gondeville's St Katherine Chapel is disputed in the absence of convincing evidence that it was once an ecclesiastical building. By the 18c it had become a meeting hall, and was for a time called the Guild Hall.

At the back of Market Square are Ardley House and Cotswold House, which form part of the last stage of building in the High Street. These, and some others, were built in the early 19c by farmers made rich by the Enclosures Act which came into force around 1800.

Campden is pleasantly free from the showy commercialism that sometimes spoils towns that have acquired reputations as showpieces. With its array of fine stone houses, it is a fitting place to

Chipping Campden: The Market Hall in the High Street

start this walk along the scarp slope of these low hills.

Campden was obviously a town of some repute from early times. In the 12c and 13c, when it was customary for the English monarchs to progress continually around the realm, Campden saw its share of royalty, with known visits from Henry II, Henry III and King John, who arrived one month after Magna Carta. Henry III also stayed at nearby Evesham as a prisoner of Simon de Montfort before being released by his son Edward.

A place of ancient traditions, the prosperity of Campden was based, as with many other towns we shall pass *en route*, on the Cotswold Lion, the long-faced Cotswold sheep. By 1300, half of England's revenue came from wool exports and Campden, which had established itself as a marketing rather than a weaving centre, received its fair share of this wealth through its rich merchants. The first of these was William Grevel, a contemporary of Chaucer and mentioned by him in the *Canterbury Tales*. Then there were the Calfs, and later Sir Baptist Hicks, co-founder of the East India Company. When the structure of the industry changed and the processing side took precedence, with the movement of the centre of gravity to the Stroud Valley, Campden's importance declined, and its profits from the wool trade were finally destroyed by the Act forbidding dealing in wool by any town not in the Inland Staple. Campden petitioned to be made a staple town, but in vain. The town then went into a quiet hibernation to which we owe its unspoilt nature. A new activity came to the town in 1902, when C.R. Ashbee was persuaded to bring his School of Arts and Crafts to Campden from London. He also restored Woolstaplers' Hall. The framework of local crafts thus created exists to this day.

Chipping Campden to Dover's Hill

The Cotswold Way continues along the High Street from the Market Hall, passing on the L Sheep Street that leads to Westington. This tiny village, almost a suburb of Campden, has picture-book rows of thatched cottages that are worth a visit if time permits. Otherwise carry on along High Street until a road goes R signed 'Back Ends and Hoo Lane'. Take this road, and soon a lane leads L signed 'Hoo Lane, Cotswold Way'. The introduction is

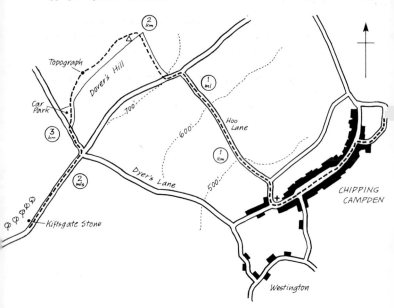

over, the signs and the walking start here. The name 'hoo' derives
from the Saxon 'hoh' (a spur of land), and this particular spur
descends from Dover's Hill above. Follow the lane and the
bridleway beyond to the road at the top. Turn L, and after a few
yards turn R through a gap in the hedge opposite. This gap is
signposted 'Dover's Hill, Aston-sub-Edge, 2km', or at least it should
be. Unfortunately some signs have a habit of pointing the wrong
way, a product either of the circular pole that allows the wind to
turn the sign or the local humorists. It is advisable to check the
maps when such signs are met.

Follow the field hedge and emerge, at the far side, on Dover's
Hill. Turn L and follow the trees past the OS trig point and then go
over to the topograph on the scarp edge. If you are a walker used to
trig points on remote peaks, the one standing by trees that overtop it
by many feet is a little comical. But even such a walker may be

impressed by the view; rarely are those from mountain peaks so expansive. The topograph itself points out the features of interest in the Vale of Evesham below and, of those at a greater distance, the view of Worcestershire's Malvern Hills is especially fine. Here the Cotswold escarpment turns E as the hills reach their northern limit, and the view along the edge at this point shows it to perfection.

Description of route continues on p. 43.

The narrow stretch of enclosed land between this scarp and the trees is of historic interest, being all that now remains of the site of the Cotswold 'Olympick' Games. The name commemorates the originator, or more likely, reviver of a tradition of sport on this site. Robert Dover was a Norfolk man who moved to the Campden area in the late 16c or early 17c. He lived, initially, at Saintbury to the W of Campden, and then at Campden itself. He practised law in London while living at Campden, and his clients included some of the more famous names of the day, the Shakespeares of Stratford and Richard Catesby, cousin of Robert Catesby of Gunpowder-Plot fame. Dover, by all accounts, was a good-natured and jovial extrovert. It is probable that some form of games had been celebrated on the hill at Whitsun from Saxon times, but the more organised events started around 1612. Dover, through his friend Endymion Porter, who was at court, obtained James I's approval of the games. James, at the time, was attempting to steer a course between the rival factions of Catholicism, Puritanism, and royal government, a course that became too difficult a few years later and ended in the Civil War. He seems to have been whole-heartedly in favour of the venture, however, despite its anti-Puritan overtones, and went so far as to give Dover, through Porter, a royal suit with hat and feather. This suit was worn by Dover when he opened the games each year. The games were held on the Thursday and Friday after Whitsun and included wrestling, 'leaping', dancing, 'pitching the bar', 'handling the pike', leap-frog and walking on the hands, together with the peculiarly Cotswold pastimes of singlestick fighting and shin-kicking. In singlestick or backsword fighting, each man held a long stick in one hand and had the other tucked into his belt. The idea of the game was to 'break the other's head', and some bouts lasted hours, with the contestants 'showing great courage and hardihood'. If singlestick fighting needed a strong head then shin-kicking required strong shins. In his *Wold Without End*, H. J. Massingham records one contestant who used to strengthen his shins by having them beaten with a deal plank, and another who performed a similar exercise on himself with a hammer!

In addition to these games there were also hare-coursing, horse-
and foot-racing and, in tents, card games and chess. It appears these
were introduced by Dover to bring a little refinement to the rough
pastimes of the peasants. The proceedings were opened by Dover in
the king's suit, riding a white horse. He had had erected a
prefabricated castle complete with flags and guns, the guns being
fired at intervals, but, with an eye to Hellenistic tradition, he also
had a man dressed as Homer, playing the harp.

In their day the games were famous. Shakespeare, who died in
1616, may have visited the games and may also have been
acquainted with Dover. He has Slender asking of Page in *The Merry
Wives of Windsor*: 'How does your fallow greyhound, Sir? I heard he
was out-run on Cotsall.' In 1636 Matthew Walbancke, a friend of
Dover's and later printer to the Long Parliament, printed *Annalia
Dubrensia – Upon the yeerely celebration of Mr. Robert Dover's
Olympick Games upon Cotswold Hills*. This was a slim volume
containing 34 poems, 33 by friends of Dover saluting him and the
games, and one by Dover himself, thanking those friends who had
compiled the book. The contributors can be divided into five
groups: older, established poets including Michael Drayton and Ben
Jonson; younger poets; admiring relatives of Dover, such as his son
John; local friends, including Francis Izod, Izod being a name
familiar to wanderers in Cotswold churchyards; and legal friends.
The original volume is now an expensive rarity, though it is of little
literary value. It is interesting however to note the relatively high
level of ability among the local gentry and Dover's legal friends. On
the first page of *Annalia Dubrensia* is depicted a man on a white
horse, arrayed in finery which includes a hat with a feather. It is
believed that this is a portrait of Dover in the act of opening the
games, and the portrait has been used for the NT memorial at the
car park beside the hill.

Also in 1636, Prince Rupert, the King's nephew, visited the games
with Endymion Porter. It appears that by then the games had
become the 'in' place for the gentry. In 1642, when Rupert was
fighting for his uncle the King, John Dover was one of his captains
of horse. The Civil War brought an end to the games for many
years. The last open battle of the war was fought in 1646 on the

slopes of Dover's Hill and on over the Cotwolds to Stow-on-the-Wold. Robert Dover himself died in 1652 and was buried at Barton-on-the-Heath, 8 miles SE of Campden.

After the Restoration, the games were revived. In May 1725 the *Gloucester Journal* advertised:

At Dover's Meeting on Campden Hill on Whitsun Thursday and Friday will be played as follows:
One Gold Ring and Six Belts to be wrestled for; One Lac'd Hat and Six Pairs of Gloves to be played at Backsword for; One Pair of Men's Shoes and One Pair of Women's Lac'd Shoes to be danc'd jigs for. All given GRATIS.

Despite criticism from the clergy, one of whom complained of the 'ridiculous gestures and acts of folly and buffoonery . . . [which] grown-up persons should be ashamed of', the games continued, the site changing its name from Campden Hill to Dover's Hill during the succeeding 100 years. By 1826 the prizes were monetary; for the singlestick fighters there was 18 shillings for the winner and 3 shillings for the loser of each of 12 pairs. By mid-century there was a general air of unpleasantness, the games having become a Mecca for pickpockets and thieves, and card-sharps in the tents. There were occasional riots, tents being levelled. In 1846–53, when the Oxford, Worcester and Wolverhampton railway was being constructed nearby, the disorders got out of hand, the railway workers running riot not only at the games but also in Campden itself. In the last couple of years, things were so bad that the locals no longer attended. Eventually, in 1853, following an act of enclosure, the land on which the games were held was divided and fenced, and the games came to an end.

In 1928, the National Trust bought what is now known as Dover's Hill, the land including part of that on which the games were held. In 1951, there was a revival, with the formation of a Robert Dover's Games Society and games are held on the eve of the Scuttlebrook Wake, on the Saturday following the Spring Bank Holiday.

Go across to the car park where the NT collection box stands with its supposed portrait of Robert Dover. Turn L from the car park and R at the crossroads along the road marked 'Willersey 2½m, Broadway 3¼m'.

About half a mile along this road on the R, hidden amongst the undergrowth and trees, is the Kiftsgate Stone, one of the more remarkable remains of the route. This marks a 'moot' place, where in earlier times the people of the surrounding district met to discuss tribal business, hold festivals, or mete out justice. Such meetings were held at a prominent spot – a tree or stone, a hill in flat country, or a specially set up wooden post. There is some evidence that such moot places were sited preferentially at track crossings, but the tracks may have sprung into existence after the site was chosen. The word 'gate' is derived from the Saxon 'geat' – a track – and only

The Kiftsgate Stone

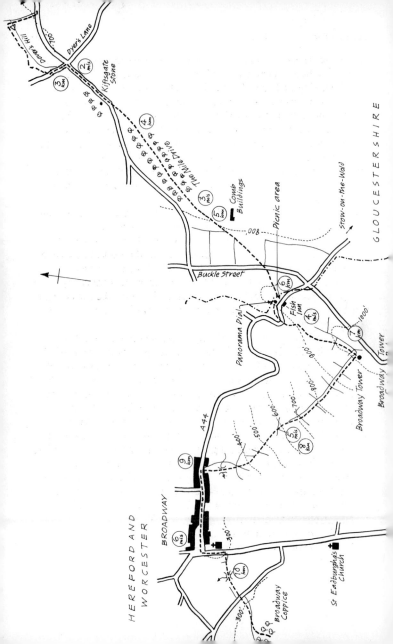

latterly has the word come to mean a barrier on such a track. In the Domesday Book the area around the stone is called the Cheftsihat Hundred, Chief's Track (?) Hundred, a hundred being an ancient land division, originally the area of land containing a hundred families, but later a sub-division of a shire. It is certain that the stone was used as a meeting-place for the Kiftsgate Hundred in Saxon times, and probably earlier. Magna Carta was read from the stone, and kings were proclaimed from it, a practice that was carried on until the proclamation of King George III, by which time the stone had been in continuous use for at least 1,200 years, possibly much longer.

Continue down the road and, on reaching the trees on the L, enter them to walk along the Mile Drive – a wide, grassy avenue that perhaps at one time led towards the stone. At the end of the drive are two fields where in the appropriate season the walker may have to negotiate a narrow path through chest-high golden wheat.

Crossing a road – part of Buckle Street, an ancient trackway – the path leads across the field to the Fish Inn, visible on the further side. Here, crossing the picnic area to the inn, the walker enters Worcestershire.

The Fish Inn is a curious building with a sundial on top. It was built by Sir John Coterill in the late 18c, but part of it is reputed to be the remnants of a 14c priest house. It was used as a gazebo and summerhouse. The name is derived from the early Christian symbol of the three fishes. In the 17c, when Broadway was established as a significant staging-post on the coach route from Worcester to Oxford and London, there was a stone near the site of the inn inscribed 'Shut off two horses here'; extra horses were taken on at the foot of Fish Hill for the long haul up to this point. The stone has since been moved, and now forms part of a gateway on Fish Hill.

Take the track that leads off the A44 on the left a little way down the hill from the Fish Inn; somewhere near here the Perrys from Campden were hanged. Soon, however, open land is reached, a curious stretch with numerous dry hollows. The track is straightforward, leading to Broadway Tower.

Description of route continues on p. 48.

Broadway Tower

Broadway Tower

The tower was constructed in 1799 by the Earl of Coventry in response, it is said, to a request from his wife. In 1797 Admiral Duncan, later Earl Camperdown, who lived at Shipston-on-Stour, gained his victory over the Dutch at the naval battle of Camperdown. In celebration, a victory bonfire was lit on the hill. The Countess of Coventry is said to have been so impressed that the bonfire could be seen from the family seat at Croome Court, Worcester, that she asked for the tower to be built as a permanent visual reminder of the family's Cotswold estate. This story may or may not be true; that period of history saw the construction of many follies, a good number of them sham castles. The tower was designed by James Wyatt, who conceived it as a 'dark' Saxon tower and had a stone darker than the local stone brought, probably from the Northamptonshire border, for its construction. Later repairs in the lighter-coloured local stone can easily be seen.

The tower is constructed on the summit of Broadway or Beacon Hill, which, at 1,024 ft, is the second highest point of the Cotswolds and is renowned for its panoramic view. The top of the 55-ft tower is in fact the highest elevation on Cotswold that can be reached easily. The panoramic view from the hilltop, sometimes said, like many others, to be the broadest in England, is not made noticeably broader by ascending the tower. At one time it was possible to see 13 counties from the top, but county boundary realignment has reduced this to 12. This view extends to May Hill to the N of the Forest of Dean and, to the R of it, the Black Mountains. Further R are the Malverns, the Clee Hills, the Wrekin in Shropshire and the Clent Hills. To the S is the next high spot on the route, Cleeve Hill. In the valleys below can be seen Broadway and, further R, Pershore with its famous Norman Abbey.

The tower was sold in 1827 to Sir Thomas Phillips of Broadway, who leased it later to two Oxford tutors, Price and Stone. At this time it was in a poor state of repair, and Carmel Price had it restored and redecorated for the princely sum of £9 in 1867. Many of his friends and students stayed at the tower, including the Pre-Raphaelites, the painter Sir Edward Burne-Jones, William Morris (who wrote the letter forming the Society for the Protection of

Ancient Buildings from the tower) and Dante Gabriel Rossetti.

The tower remained a private dwelling until 1972, since when it has become the focal point of the Broadway Tower Country Park. The tower itself was renovated and houses exhibitions on its first and second floors. The third floor has a profile map of the surrounding area, and above it is a viewing gallery.

In addition to the tower, there are two further buildings, the Rookery Barn which houses the information centre, and the Tower Barn, which contains further exhibits. Tower Barn, a typical Cotswold field barn, is about 150 years old. Such barns were built without foundations, and have relatively steep-angled roofs to take the weight of the stone roof-tiles, which are very much heavier than slate tiles. Note also the triangular holes in the walls, provided both for ventilation and to allow access for barn owls to assist the farmer by catching mice. The exhibits illustrate the local country crafts such as dry-stone walling and roofing, together with the geology and natural history of the area. There are also two short nature walks, one taking about 30 minutes of trail, on which guided tours are available, and one taking about an hour.

The Broadway Tower Country Park, owned by the Batsford Estates Company, with grants from the Countryside Commission, is open every day from April to September and, at weekends only, from October until March.

Broadway Tower to Broadway

The route runs slightly N of W from the tower downhill towards Broadway, which is visible in the valley below. The way is obvious, keeping the hedge and wall to the R and losing height rapidly. When an open field is at last reached, the waymarker arrows, after a prominent ash tree has been passed, point in two directions. The best view of Broadway is given by following those with dots above them, which trend diagonally R across the field, leading over a footbridge and out into Broadway High Street.

Description of route continues on p. 56.

Broadway is a village with which the first-time visitor falls in, or
out of, love instantly. It has no special place in history, or other
reasons for its renown, and yet in its buildings can be seen the
history of man in the Cotswolds. It is proud of its unspoilt nature,
yet it has an abundance of antique shops, tea shops, refreshment
and souvenir centres. It has a village green – one of the few village
greens left on the Cotswold Edge – yet there is nowhere you can
walk without bumping into cars, and nothing you can look at
without peering over a river of painted metal. Some hardly care to
go anywhere else, and some prefer never to come again.

The village is split into two, the old church being about a mile
away from the main village along the Snowshill road. The main
street of the village itself is of surprising width. The reason for this
is that two streams ran down it, one on each side, until they were
piped, in the mid-19c. Some dip-holes for buckets remained, and
these were filled in within living memory. The streams were flanked
by willows, with the houses beyond. The name Broadway (given to
the village because of the unusual width of its main street) was
originally Bradanwega, later Bradweg, the local pronunciation being
Brodey.

There has been a village in the area since very early times. The old
church is dated around 1160, and the oldest building in the main
village is the Abbot's Grange, situated below the green behind a yew
screen. This house was constructed around 1320 for use by the
Abbots of Pershore, who owned Broadway. Though restored later,
it still contains much of the original work, including a hall and
chapel. Prior's Manse, the opposite side from which the Cotswold
Way enters Broadway, is believed to be as old as the Grange. It is
thought to have been constructed for a Prior of Worcester, and is
remarkable for its 'modern' look, with high gables and dormer
windows. The Grange and Manse are amongst the oldest houses in
Worcestershire. Many others date from the mid-15c onwards, but
much rebuilding has taken place since that time, particularly in the
17c and 18c, when Broadway was at its height in commercial terms,
and in more recent times when it was 'discovered' as a centre for
Cotswold tourism.

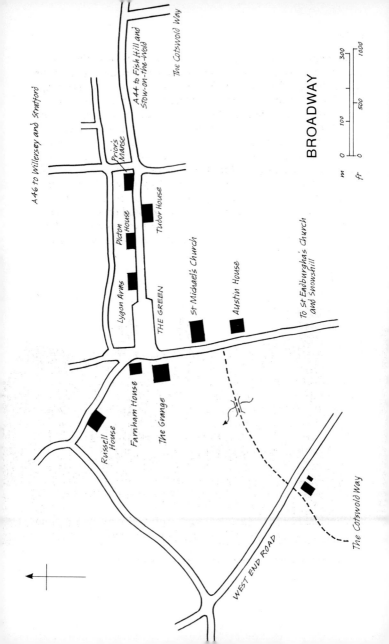

BROADWAY

A46 to Willersey and Stratford

A44 to Fish Hill and Stow-on-the-Wold

The Cotswold Way

Prior's Manse

Picton House

Tudor House

Lygon Arms

THE GREEN

St Michael's Church

Austin House

To St Eadburgha's Church and Snowshill

Russell House

Farnham House

The Grange

WEST END ROAD

The Cotswold Way

m

ft

0   100   300

0   500   1000

The commercial success of the 17c and 18c was due to the stage coach plying between London and Worcester. Broadway was on the main route from Worcester to Oxford, and there was much coming and going of Royalist and Parliamentary troops in the Civil War. King Charles spent a night at Broadway Court in 1641, and a room in the then White Horse Inn, now the Lygon Arms, is named after Oliver Cromwell. Success as a staging-post on the trip to London was based on two factors: the steepness of Fish Hill, which necessitated the taking on of fresh, and extra horses, and a piece of inspired business by the butler of General Lygon, who lived on the Springhill Estate. Seeing the likely importance of Broadway, he bought the White Horse Inn from the General and renamed it the Lygon Arms, ostensibly to mark the General's contribution to the victory at Waterloo but also in order to use the coat-of-arms as a

Broadway: The 14c Prior's Manse, one of the oldest houses in Worcestershire

Broadway: The Lygon Arms, one of the original coaching inns

sign, and made a fortune. Soon the village possessed more than 20 coaching inns. The boom lasted until the coming of the railway.

But still the village prospered, for this was the time of its discovery, or perhaps rediscovery. The fame, or blame, for this must lie with William Morris who, as we have already seen, spent time as a guest at Broadway Tower. Following his recommendations Frank Millet, an artist, came to the village and was immediately captivated. He rented Farnham House beside the Grange, where he lived until his death in the *Titanic* disaster, and from there encouraged a variety of artists to visit. He also used the Abbot's Grange as a studio. In the wake of the artists came others: J. M. Barrie, Vaughan Williams and Edward Elgar. The American actress Mary Anderson de Navarro settled here, as did Lady Maud Bowes-Lyon, aunt of Queen Elizabeth the Queen Mother.

Whatever adverse feelings may be aroused by the commercialisation of the village, its architectural delights are

Broadway: The green

undeniable. The line of cottages on the N side of the green, for
instance, consists of fine Cotswold dwellings of the late 16c and 17c,
showing the typical local features of high gables, ornamental
chimneys and drip mouldings, with steep-angled stone-tiled roofs.
Picton House, further up the Way from the Lygon Arms, is a good
example of the next stage of development in the 18c. The gables are
now absent, as are the drip moulds, and the development of cheap
glass-making has allowed the designer to use larger windows.
Another interesting house of this period is Austin House, beside the
new church.

If Broadway shows many of the interesting developments in
Cotswold architecture, its inhabitants have also shown many aspects
of English eccentricity. Lord Coventry started it all with the tower,
and General Lygon continued the process. While living on the
Springhill Estate, he not only sold his butler the White Horse Inn
but also planted the estate with clumps of beech trees following the

pattern of the main bodies of troops at the battle of Waterloo. Later Sir Thomas Phillips set up home in Middle Hill. While at Rugby School, he started to collect books and manuscripts and continued after moving to Broadway, declaring it his intention to own a copy of every book in the world. He employed a printer to work at the tower printing old manuscripts, but the man would not stay there, saying that the place was too damp and decayed, with its broken windows and collapsed ceilings. When Phillips died in 1872, his collection represented the greatest private library in existence, reputedly filling 4 rooms, 250 boxes and 103 waggons.

The new church near the green was built in 1840 to avoid the long walk from the village to the old church. It is an undistinguished building, whose only true treasure, a beautifully carved and canopied Jacobean pulpit, was brought here from the old church.

The old church itself is not on the route but is worth a detour. It

Broadway: A typical Cotswold cottage

has been rebuilt and refurbished several times since its original construction in the late 12c. It is dedicated to St Eadburgha, a granddaugher of King Alfred who spent most of her life in the nunnery of Nunnaminster near Winchester until her death as its Abbess in 960. When Egilwold, the Earl of Dorset, rebuilt the monastery at Pershore, he received part of the relics of Eadburgha, which were richly enshrined. The shrine was the source of many miracles, and when the Broadway church was founded it was natural to place it under St Eadburgha's protection.

Consequent upon the building of the new church in the mid-19c. St Eadburgha escaped the Victorian reconstruction of many such churches. It stands beautifully amongst the trees, cruciform, with the tower dividing nave from chancel. It is little used now, but is open to the public and maintained in perfect order. The stones in the wall to the side of the gate may be an old horse-mounting station. The

Broadway: The 12c church of St Eadburgha, about 1 mile from the Cotswold Way

interior contains the original Norman aisle arcades and a plain Norman font. There is beautiful Jacobean woodwork, though the pulpit is gone. Gone also are several brasses, one of those that remain commemorating Sir Anthony Dastyn, Sheriff of Worcester and lord of the manor of Broadway until his death in 1572. The memorial is unusual in being engraved on the reverse of half of a more ancient one, the other half being in Westerham, Kent. Another memorial is inscribed:

As thow art so was I
As I am so shalt thow bee

Broadway to Stanton and Stanway

The Way leaves Broadway along the lane opposite the new church. Cross the fields and stream and emerge on the minor road. Here the route is not well marked, but is none the less obvious. Cross the road, go over the stile and follow the hedge up to a gate, and then go diagonally up across the field to a wood – Broadway Coppice. Before entering the wood, turn to take one last look at the village below. Viewed from here, when the tourist traps cannot be seen, it looks delightful.

Now take the track through the wood, which can be unpleasantly muddy in wet weather. At the exit from the wood, the Way leads on through farm buildings; care must be taken to stay on the route so as to avoid antagonising the local farmers. The Way is well signed, however, through cream-painted gates and barns. Here we re-enter Gloucestershire. Eventually a long, straight farm-track is reached that gives boring walking, but fine views L of Broadway Tower. It ends at a gate marked 'Croghan Hill Farm', where a stile leads to a track signposted 'Shenberrow Hill, Stanton'. A spring L offers good drinking water. On the R we have a glimpse of the village of Buckland, superbly placed in the valley below. Buckland is the first of the series of fine villages at the scarp base between Broadway and Winchcombe.

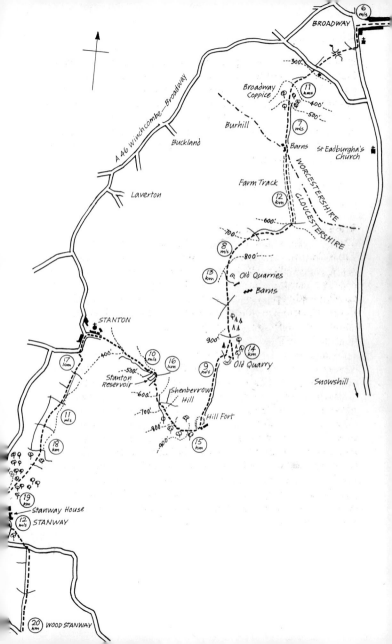

The Way continues past a series of old quarries to a gate between stone walls. Just beyond here the official route goes straight on through some inelegant woodland and then moves back R on a broader track. This might be avoided by going R from the gate. Whichever way is taken, a large quarry is reached. Here a gate marked 'Shenberrow Farm' leads by a wide, stony track to the farm and hill fort.

The hill fort at Shenberrow is the first of many that will be passed on the Way, though it is not one of the best. The forts are of Iron-Age construction, built between 700 BC and 150 BC. They were initially used as defensive positions in which the local community could take refuge when threatened by marauders. The earliest types had a simple ditch and rampart. Later designs were multi-vallate–that is, composed of a number of such rampart/ditch defences. It is not clear whether the evolution of the multiple defences caused, or was caused by, the invention of the sling-shot, which allowed long-range bombardment of the defenders. Later forts were made large enough to contain whole villages.

Shenberrow is a typical bi-vallate site covering about 3 acres. The name is, however, atypical. The normal suffix for such places is 'bury', from 'burh' (a camp or fortified hill). In the present case the suffix is from 'bearg' (a hill), 'shen' being probably derived from 'scene' (beautiful). The fort has suffered much from the destruction of its ramparts, though, after passing through it and taking the path down through the woods, the full effectiveness of the natural W scarp slope can be seen. When complete it must have been a formidable place, occupying, as it does, a position above the 900-ft contour.

Follow the track down through the wood, watching for waymarkers on the trees. The track is steep, and can be muddy, but the wood is quiet and shady in summer. When the track levels out, care must be taken to follow the waymarked path going L rather than to continue R on the more obvious one. On emerging from the wood into a field, avoid the temptation to wander too far from the fence on the R because of the fallen trees; the route switches from one side of the hedge to the other after passing an old ruined building. Continue on down to Stanton reservoir, and pass round to the R. This section is very muddy in wet weather. Stanton village is entered by a sign 'Shenberrow Hill 1 km, Broadway 6.5 km'.

Description of route continues on p. 63.

Stanton, and its sister-village Stanway, are the untarnished jewels of
the northern part of the Way, with their rows of completely unspoilt
houses, many of great interest. Stanton derives from 'Stan Tun' –
stony farm – and stone there is, in marvellous abundance. Most of
the houses are from the early 17c, but their present condition is due
to Sir Philip Stott, an architect, who, between 1900 and his death in
1937, spent most of his time and money restoring them to their
original state. A particularly fine building is Stanton Court, which
was extended and renovated in the early 17c by Henry Izod. The
Izods were an important family in the area, having moved here from
Chapel Izod in County Kilkenny, around 1450. Another fine house is
Stanton Manor, also known as Warren House. The latter name
derives from an extension added, according to the date-stone, in
1577 by Thomas Warren, although much of the house is older.

The church is reached by a short diversion to the R at the cross
in the main street, which has an 18c shaft in a medieval base. The

Stanton: The main street and medieval village cross

Stanton: The doorway of St Michael's Church

Stanton: The organ gallery and font, St Michael's Church

church is built on the site of an early Saxon church, possibly of wood, since nothing of it remains. The earliest parts of the existing church are Norman in style and date from the 12c. Most of the building – the tower and spire, S aisle and porch – was constructed in the 15c, when the church was also extended westwards. In the room above the porch is one of the smallest museums in the country, containing, amongst other things, a hay-rake, a warming pan, an old press and a pair of old pattens.

The interior has some interesting features. The deep gouges in the pew ends were made by dog chains. There are two pulpits, the older being one of the few surviving 14c English wooden pulpits. It is a pity it has become so defaced. The newer one is of the 17c; it is thought that John Wesley preached from it. The E window contains some fragments of ancient glass, including a white rose and two apostles.

Stanton to Stanway

The route is rejoined by passing again through the neat churchyard. The ancient tombs commemorate the families who built the largest houses: the Izods, the Wynniates who succeeded them, and the Warrens. Follow the main street around L and leave it at one of the thoughtfully integrated street lamps where a signpost, 'Shenberrow Hill 1·5 km, Snowshill 3·5 km, Stanway 2 km' points past a gate marked 'Chestnut Farm only'. Pass through this gate and a sign post marked 'Stanway' is soon reached. The route traverses fields below the scarp slope to emerge on the road again just outside Stanway. *Description of route continues on p. 67.*

Stanway

The name of the village is derived from 'Stan-weg' or 'stony way', describing the road that runs through it. The route emerges on the road opposite a cricket pavilion – a thatched building set up, barn-like, on staddle stones. This was a gift to the village from Sir James Barrie, who was a cricket fanatic and at one time lived in nearby Stanway House. Staddle stones are a renowned feature of Cotswold barns.

The house itself is seen a little further up the road towards the

Stanway: The cricket pavilion

village, behind signs marked 'Not open to the Public'. With its three storeys and four gables, it has an elegance of line that is the equal of anything met elsewhere on the Way. It was built by Sir Paul Tracy, who died in 1620, in the reign of James I. Architecturally it is a dignified mansion of the early Renaissance, the W front being particularly fine. The house was one of the last domestic residences to be built with a great hall; from that date the owners retired to their private quarters and stopped eating with the servants. The hall has an oriel window divided into 60 panes and reaching almost to the roof eaves. The mansion has had an eventful history, having been much modified over the centuries, particularly in the 19c and 20c, when additions were made. In 1948 many of these were pulled down, and what remains is chiefly original, with some 18c and 19c extras rather than modifications.

The eventful history of the building has been shared by some of

Stanway: The south gate of Stanway House

the occupants. The builder himself was one of remarkable stock. Sir William Tracy, who died in 1530, was a Protestant when the country was still Catholic, and left a will that was so markedly Protestant that it was deemed heretical by the Archbishop of Canterbury. The perpetrator of the heresy was dead, but the Archbishop ordered that the body be exhumed and burnt at the stake. Things had come full circle a few years later when Sir William's son, Richard, assisted in the dissolution of the Catholic religious houses. It was Richard Tracy who delivered the Hailes Blood (which will be mentioned later) to London for analysis.

The house was also the home of Dr Robert Dover, grandson of Robert, of Olympick Games fame. Dr Dover was known as the Quicksilver Doctor, from a mercury-based medicine he devised that sounds far worse than any of the diseases it was designed to cure. He was a man of eccentric habits, being a privateer around the turn

of the 18c, and was captain of the ship that rescued Alexander
Selkirk, the original of Robinson Crusoe, from the island of Juan
Fernandez in 1708. He was buried in Stanway in 1742.

Near the house stands a massive tithe barn complete with
buttresses, cart porch and the traditional steep stone-slated roof. The
barn, which was built certainly in the 15c and possibly the 14c, is
now privately owned.

The route follows the road round its right-angle through the
lower village. Here stands, next to the simple 12c church, the S gate
of Stanway House. It was at one time believed to be the work of
Inigo Jones, but is now thought to have been built after his style by
Timothy Strong of Taynton. With its exaggerated proportions, it is
strangely placed, butted against the high house wall, and appears
ostentatious beside the church.

The church was rebuilt in the 12c, replacing the one mentioned in

Stanway: The tithe barn

the Domesday survey. The tower was added in the 13c. Sadly, much of the original work was destroyed in a burst of enthusiastic rebuilding around 1900. The original stone was used to construct the N wall of the churchyard in the fifties of this century. Fortunately the Victorian rebuilding did not entirely destroy the church's basic, simple character.

Stanway to Hailes Abbey

Leaving Stanway, the Way follows an easily recognisable route to the hamlet of Wood Stanway, so called to distinguish it from the village we have just left. Stanway itself was once called Church Stanway to distinguish it from its neighbour. The hamlet is beautifully situated, protected on three sides by the scarp and possessed of a collection of plain stone cottages and farms. The fruit-trees thrive in this sheltered site with its western outlook, and in spring, when the blossom is out, the setting is idyllic.

From it, the Way climbs steeply some 400 ft to the scarp summit at Stumps Cross, passing the farmhouse where stood once the summer residence of the Abbot of Hailes. The route starts along the road signposted 'Stanway Estate. Vehicles to Glebe Farm only. Footpath to Coscombe and Stumps Cross'. It is easily followed, as it is well waymarked and runs initially parallel to the power lines.

Emerging on to the B4077 at the end of the Coscombe farm drive, turn R, crossing to the L side of the road as soon as possible to minimise the dangers of the blind, downhill bend. At the top of the hill is Stumps Cross, the stump itself being set forlornly by the post-box in the wall R. The cross was probably medieval, following a tradition of placing these crosses at the summits of very long or steep hills so that the traveller could thank God the climb was over.

East of here, at Temple Guiting, is a feature well removed from the route that nevertheless deserves mention: the Cotswold Farm Park. Open between mid-May and the end of September, from 10.30 to 18.00, the park contains the finest display of rare breeds of British farm animals to be seen in the country. The aim of the park is to breed as well as to show the animals, and as such it works closely with the Rare Breeds Survival Trust. Included in the breeds on show are descendants of the original Cotswold sheep on whose

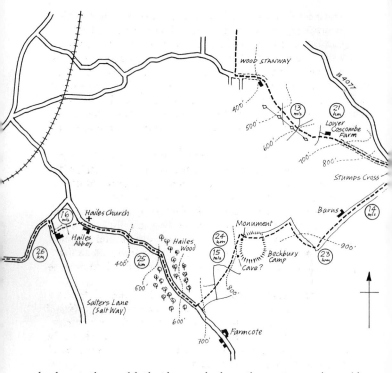

back rests the wealth that has made the entire route so unique. Also here are the Orkney sheep, who can survive on storm-lashed seashores by eating seaweed, and the Soay, small and brown – the original Iron-Age sheep. The cows include the Old Gloucester whose milk was used for the original Double Gloucester Cheese. There are also rare pigs, including the Gloucester Old Spot and the Tamworth Ginger, and rare fowls.

The Way from Stumps Cross follows the path signposted 'Farmcote 2·5 km, Hailes Abbey 3 km, Winchcombe 6 km', and soon passes an interesting amalgam of old and new techniques, a barn R being of metal, but set up on staddle stones.

The route continues across farmland to Beckbury Camp, a hill fort that originally consisted of a single ditch and rampart. The ditch has long since been filled in, but the rampart is still clearly visible, particularly on the E side, the side of approach, where it is still very steep, giving a good idea of the original appearance. The enclosed land is about 4 acres. The W side of the fort, below which the route runs, has been constructed along the natural scarp line to enhance the defences, and the fort commands an outstanding view of the surrounding countryside so that ample time to prepare for attack was available.

Before traversing the lower W rampart, the route passes in the NW corner a stone structure some 10 ft high and 2 ft square, with recesses that might have contained statues. There is no hint of any inscription, or any other reason for its existence.

When traversing the W rampart, it is advisable to stay above the water-trough in the field below, since the ground below it becomes very boggy. The upper traverse allows a view of a second curious and unexplained feature, a triangular cave with dry-stone walling, stone and wooden lintels and evidence of old hinging for a door no longer there.

The Way descends to the track that leads off R through Hailes Wood towards the abbey. This path offers fine views of the ruins of the abbey itself, and of Hailes Church. Soon the abbey is reached.

In view of the historic interest of the ruins, and of the other abbey at nearby Winchcombe, it seems in order here to give some general background on these religious houses.

Description of route follows on p. 80.

HAILES ABBEY

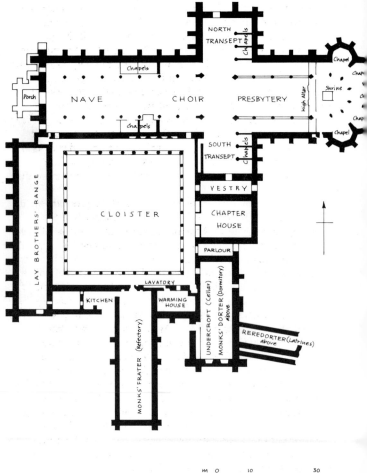

NORTH TRANSEPT

Chapels

Chapels

Chapels

Chapel

Chapel

Chapel

Shrine

High Altar

PRESBYTERY

CHOIR

NAVE

Porch

Chapels

chapels

SOUTH TRANSEPT

Chapels

VESTRY

CHAPTER HOUSE

PARLOUR

LAY BROTHERS' RANGE

CLOISTER

LAVATORY

KITCHEN

WARMING HOUSE

UNDERCROFT (Cellar)

MONKS' DORTER (Dormitory) above

REREDORTER (Latrines) above

MONKS' FRATER (Refectory)

m 0   10   30
ft 0   50   100

In early 1536 there were almost 1,000 monasteries and nunneries in England and Wales in which lived some 17,000 men and women in holy orders. And yet the monastic system was not at its height. There was a history of monasticism stretching back to St Augustine and his colleagues at Canterbury in the late 6c, and periodic revivals – notably at the time of the Norman Conquest and again in the 13c – led to the peak of monastic achievement around 1300. Despite building work after that date, the tendency had been for the population of monks and nuns to decline, owing, in part, to a falling off in the numbers of those offering themselves to the life, and in part to the Black Death of the 14c, which had decimated monks and laymen alike. By 1536 the great abbeys were declining both in importance and in their population of monks, some being more than half empty.

It is difficult at this distance from the times of the great abbeys in the 13c to realise the importance of such establishments to the surrounding communities. The major function and responsibility of such houses was the maintenance of prayer. To this end, the day of the monks was punctuated by attendance at mass. Even their sleep was broken by the prayers of the night office. In theory the monks lived the harshest of lives, in abject poverty, with no possessions, cut off from their fellow men, and they had taken a vow of celibacy. Their lives were ostensibly passed in an endless round of penance for sin and absolving prayer. They gave the peasant, who had to work too hard to spend all his day praying, hope for salvation through their suffering. The monks also looked after, with due reverence, the saintly relics enshrined in the house, to which the peasant could make pilgrimage to gain personal absolution. On the face of it, the system worked well, and to the profit of all sides. The peasantry, for the relatively small price of the upkeep of a few holy men, got eternal salvation; the monks had the freedom to follow their vocations without fear of starvation; and the gentry were satisfied that the peasants had something at the centre of their lives to keep their minds off the injustices of life.

By the early 16c all was not well, however. In the course of time, the abbeys, though the individual monks lived in poverty, had become as institutions rich and, in the case of some of the larger houses, very rich indeed. As a result of frequent grants of lands and manors, the houses had become large, landowners gaining considerable incomes from the renting of farms and the sharing of profits. The abbots were more and more called upon to be estate managers and, as they became part of the landed aristocracy, to assist in actual government. Abbots sat in the upper house of Parliament. As a result of this enhanced status, many of the abbots left their simple quarters in the abbey for more sumptuous abodes adjacent to the sites. Such moves did not endear the houses to the downtrodden peasantry. As we shall see later, on reaching Winchcombe, open hostility between the locals and the monks was not uncommon. The time was ripe for the decline in the size and importance of the monastic community to be hastened. It needed only a man to come to power who could see the moment had come to reduce the power of the monastic houses, and at the same time add to his own wealth by the confiscation of their lands. That man was Henry VIII.

Henry had already, by 1536, freed himself from the possibility of a papal backlash by the 1534 act, after his divorce from Katherine of Aragon, requiring all men to take an oath agreeing to the validity of his marriage to Anne Boleyn. Men had died for their refusal to take the oath – notably Sir Thomas More, but also some Carthusian monks and Franciscan friars – but most preferred life to death, and incipient revolution seemed unlikely.

In 1536, the Suppression Act was passed. It was presented not as an act of confiscation but more one of redistribution. Since the larger houses were half-empty, the smaller houses were to be closed and the brethren moved into the larger ones. Evidence was presented of immorality in the smaller houses, royal visitors reporting on the 'manifest sin, vicious, carnal and abominable living . . . used and committed amongst the little and small abbeys'. The heads of the houses were given pensions, and the brethren were allowed either to move to larger houses or to receive a dispensation from their vows and return to normal life. The ease with which many brethren, both under this act and later in the final Dissolution, returned to the world suggests that a high percentage of them had no great enthusiasm for the monastic life.

Hailes: The abbey ruins

This first attempt at Dissolution did not go unchallenged, the
northern rebellion, or Pilgrimage of Grace, in late 1536 being the
major protest, but by the end of 1536 Henry had managed to get
rid of about a third of the houses. The northern rebellion was
suppressed with the help of Gloucestershire troops and of Sir
Anthony Kingston, lord of the manor of Painswick; and some of
the larger houses in the north were suppressed as a reprisal, the
abbots being executed for treason. Encouraged by the lack of
organised resistance, Henry felt that it was time for an attack based,
not on the immorality and over-subscription of the religious houses,
but on monasticism itself. The scene was set by the 'voluntary
surrender' of the Cluniac priory of Lewes in November 1537. The
monks declared that the monastic way of life was a superstitious
round of 'dumb ceremonies' which they were pleased to abandon in
favour of 'true Christian' lives outside the house. This set the

pattern for other surrenders, which were legalised retrospectively by an Act of Parliament in 1539. To encourage surrender, reasonably generous pensions were offered initially. As the terms became less generous, the surrenders accelerated. In March 1540 Waltham Abbey surrendered and 1,000 years of monasticism was at an end.

For the most part, the abbeys were sold off, having first been stripped of plate, bells and the lead of the roofs. Deprived of their roofs, the abbey buildings rapidly fell into decay, a fate accelerated by the wholesale looting of the stone for farm buildings and walls. Only the shells now remain. One such shell is the remains of Hailes Abbey.

In 1242 Richard, Earl of Cornwall, was returning to England from a crusade in the Holy Land. The ship carrying him was in grave danger of being wrecked off the Scillies and Richard vowed that if his life was spared he would build an abbey. The ship was not wrecked and, true to his word, Richard commenced building at Hailes in 1245 on land granted to him by his brother Henry III specifically for the fulfilment of his vow. The Abbey was dedicated on 9 November 1251 at a ceremony attended by both Henry and Queen Eleanor and an array of bishops. The ceremony, it is recorded, was exceptional both for its splendour and for the distinction of its congregation. To form the religious community, monks were sent from the Cistercian Abbey of Beaulieu. Although the Cistercians were a new order, formed in 1098 in the forest of Citeaux (Cistercium) in Burgundy, Hailes was one of the last abbeys of the order formed in England. The order was a branch of the Benedictines whose life style was based on hard work, leaving little time for leisure and idleness. Seven hours each day were devoted to religious exercises, with the rest of the time spent at work, chiefly agricultural.

Richard, Earl of Cornwall, maintained an interest in the Abbey throughout his life. In 1256 the princes of the Holy Roman Empire elected him King of the Romans and he reigned as head of the Empire for 14 years. In 1261 his wife Sanchia died and her body was buried at Hailes. Richard himself died in 1272 and his body was buried next to that of his Queen. His heart was buried at the 'mother' Abbey of Beaulieu.

Before Richard's death, the relic that was to bring Hailes almost 300 years of fame and prosperity, a phial of Christ's blood, was presented to the Abbey. One story of its origin was that its contents were abstracted by Richard's second son Edmund, when he visited the German court with his father, from a golden phial that had been sent as a present to Charlemagne from Greece. Another version is that he bought the phial from the Court of Flanders. It is certainly true that in 1270 Edmund presented a phial of the Holy Blood to Hailes, another similar phial having gone to Ashbridge where Edmund had built an abbey himself. The Holy Blood was a well-authenticated relic, being vouched for by Jacques Pantaleon, Patriarch of Jerusalem, later Pope Urban IV. Edmund followed up this gift in 1295 by presenting to the Abbey a gold cross with an enamel base containing a splinter from the True Cross. Though this second relic was important, the Holy Blood had the greater fame, and the possession of it made Hailes one of England's greatest centres for pilgrims. Chaucer has a pardoner swear 'by the blode of Christ that is in Hayles'. The Holy Blood was enshrined in a structure measuring, as excavated, 10 ft by 8 ft. Since only the base has been found, there is no evidence of its appearance, apart from the discovery of some finely carved stones which are believed to have formed part of it. Behind the shrine was an arc of 5 semi-decagonal chapels, possibly symbolic of the crown of thorns. Such an arrangement, known as a chevet – an apse with radiating chapels – was a rare feature in English monasteries, although it was in favour on the Continent. Its function was to give the relic a dignified setting, and to allow space around the shrine for the pilgrims and for religious ceremony.

For the rest, the Abbey was typical Cistercian. The church itself was over 340 ft long and 60 ft wide. There was probably a tower on the church at the crossing of the nave and transepts. The church was divided into three sections, not counting the chevet of chapels and shrine. To the W was the lay-brothers' quire, with its own altar at the eastern end. Lay-brothers were monks not in Holy Orders who performed manual duties. Next came the single-screened bay for the old and infirm monks, and finally the monks' quire, with a presbytery, the part reserved for the officiating brothers, containing the high altar. From the S transept, a door led to the vestry, and beyond the vestry was the chapter house. Here the monks met in community to discuss common business or to listen to readings from the Rules of St Benedict. Beyond the chapter house was the parlour, the only room where conversation was permitted, a Cistercian abbey being a silent house. Next came the undercroft, a cellar at ground level above which was the monks' dorter or dormitory. Leading off from the dorter was the reredorter containing the latrines. These buildings, from S transept to undercroft, formed the E side of the cloister, the central square or rectangular courtyard that was the heart of an abbey. The Hailes cloister was ten bays or archways square. Such arch-edged cloisters are the most recognisable feature to the non-specialist.

To the S of the cloister was, in the E corner, the warming room, the only place, other than the kitchen and infirmary, where a fire was allowed. Further W was a lavatory or washing room and then the monk's frater or dining room. This was a large, rectangular building, 116 ft by 30 ft, with the short side opening on the cloister by way of a moulded doorway built of a mixture of blue lias and the contrasting oolite stone. Next to the frater was the kitchen. The W side of the cloister was the lay-brothers' range, with similar facilities to those of the monks. The infirmary was to the E of the undercroft.

As with most of the English abbeys, the building at Hailes was spread over a very wide period. Indeed the cloister at the Dissolution was from the 15c rather than the 13c. In 1271 fire destroyed a large portion of the Abbey, and disaster struck again in 1337 when the fishpond burst its banks so that large parts of the Abbey were damaged. The monks were nearly wiped out by the Black Death in 1361, and the Abbey was broken into in 1364, by 'satellites of Satan' who stole some silver from the altar. The Abbey was also plagued by financial problems. Severe deficits that came to light in 1412 were put down to the vagaries of Abbot Henry, who had departed under a cloud and, to alleviate them, the Pope gave permission for the Abbey to grant relaxation worth eleven years and thirty-five days of penance to those who contributed money to the Abbey. A further grant of indulgences to contributing pilgrims followed in 1431, and the fortunes of the Abbey then remained high until the Dissolution.

The Abbey's end came late in the Dissolution. Abbot Sagar and the 21 monks who were all that remained of the community surrendered the Abbey on Christmas Eve, 1539. Before the surrender, the suppression of shrines had resulted in the confiscation of the Holy Blood in October by Richard Tracy, who was in the family line of the builder of Stanway House. The relic was taken to London for examination. In the words of Bishop Latimer of Worcester, the examiners 'thought, deemed and judged' that 'the substance and matter of the supposed relic (was) an unctuous gum coloured, which, being in the glass (the Holy Blood was enclosed in a round beryl, garnished with silver), appeared to be a glistering red, resembling partly the colour of blood; and after we did take out part of the said substance and matter out of the glass, then it was apparent glistering yellow colour, like amber or base gold and doth cleave to, as gum or bird-lime'. On 24 November Bishop Hilsey of Rochester preached publicly at St Paul's Cross and displayed the relic. He declared that it was 'honey clarified and coloured with saffron, as has been evidently proved before the King and his Council'. The relic was then destroyed.

It was claimed that the container had formed part of an elaborate hoax to deprive penitents of their funds. The monks, it was said, contended that a man in mortal sin could not see the Holy Blood, whereas one who had been absolved could. The glass vessel containing the Blood had one side thicker than the other, which rendered it opaque. At first the penitent was shown this opaque side, and only when he had paid a sufficient sum was the container turned so that the Blood came into view.

Following the surrender, the Abbey was stripped of its plate and ornaments and sold, in 1542, to a private dealer. Soon afterwards, the church was demolished, though the rest of the building remained intact. In the 17c the W range was used as a private house by the Tracy family, and in the early 18c as a pair of farmhouses. By the mid-18c, however, this last surviving remnant was demolished to provide building material for farms in the area.

The Abbey remains came under the guardianship of the government in 1948 and have been gradually re-excavated. Much of the foundation work has been exposed to give an idea of the size of the various parts of the Abbey and the position of the shrine, but three of the cloister arcades and some cloister walling on the N, W the E sides are all that remain above ground level. None the less there is sufficient to give a good idea of the majesty that the Abbey must have possessed when its buildings were complete.

In addition to the site, there is also a museum with exhibits detailing the history of the Abbey before and after the Dissolution. Some of the carved stonework shows the high degree of craftmanship and the loving care that the masons invested in the work.

Hailes Abbey is open as follows:

	Weekdays	Sundays
March and April	09.30 – 17.30	14.00 – 17.30
May to September	09.30 – 19.00	14.00 – 19.00
October	09.30 – 17.30	14.00 – 17.30
November to February	09.30 – 16.00	14.00 – 16.00

The site is closed on Christmas Eve and Day, and Boxing Day. Admission is 30p for adults, 15p for senior citizens and children.

Opposite the Abbey, partially hidden behind a clump of trees, is Hailes Church, whose treasures are, in their way, as fine as those possessed by the Abbey. The church was built in the 12c, before the Abbey, though it was extensively rebuilt in the 14c. Its beautiful medieval wall-paintings, of which it has the largest display that remains in any of the Cotswold churches, have been restored and preserved with the help of grants from the Pilgrim Trust and the Historic Churches Preservation Trust. Those near the sanctuary are in the best state of preservation. Noteworthy are the collection of heraldic symbols and scriptural friezes; the gryphons and unicorn on the southern wall; and St Catherine of Alexandria stepping on the Emperor Maximin on the northern wall. But the best finds are the small ones, those that are not part of the larger works. Look, for instance, at the beautiful brown owl on the lower S wall. In the nave, two huge murals have been the subject of much restoration. These were badly affected by later plaster work (the paintings are believed to be 14c), which may have been deliberate, later eras

Hailes: The 12c church (above) and a detail of the medieval wall paintings in the church (below)

believing such paintings to be idolatrous. That on the the N wall has a 'Good Shepherd' figure apparently carrying a small boy, and some fish symbols. That on the southern wall is a total departure from orthodoxy, being a hunting scene with three dogs and a hunter with shield closing in on a rabbit cowering below a tree. This work is remarkable, not even the dullness of the present colouring diminishing the vibrant fluidity of the painting.

Hailes Abbey to Winchcombe

Leaving the church, we head off across a field towards Winchcombe, now only 3 km distant. The path from Hailes to Winchcombe, the Pilgrims' Way, was once paved. Soon we pass a line of oak trees, very gnarled and obviously extremely old. The Way continues across pleasant countryside until a barn is reached. After that, the Way is exceedingly muddy, even when it becomes a track, but it improves eventually when Puck Pit Lane is reached. Continue down to the main road, turn L and enter Winchcombe.

Description of route continues on p. 99.

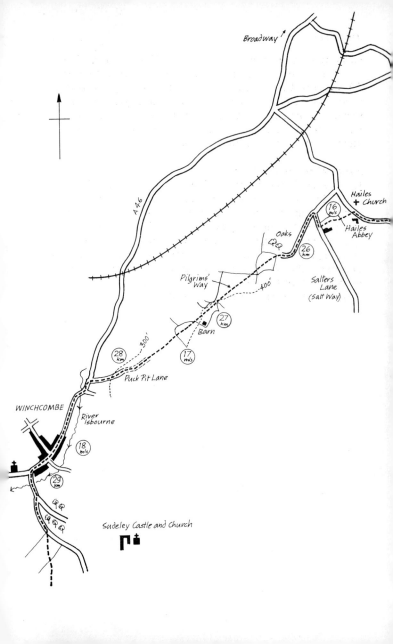

Broadway ↑

A 46

Hailes
✝ Church

Hailes
Abbey

16
mls

Oaks

26
km

Salters
Lane
(Salt Way)

Pilgrims'
Way

400'

27
km

Barn

17
mls

28
km

300'

Puck Pit Lane

WINCHCOMBE

River
Isbourne

18
mls

29
km

Sudeley Castle and Church

WINCHCOMBE

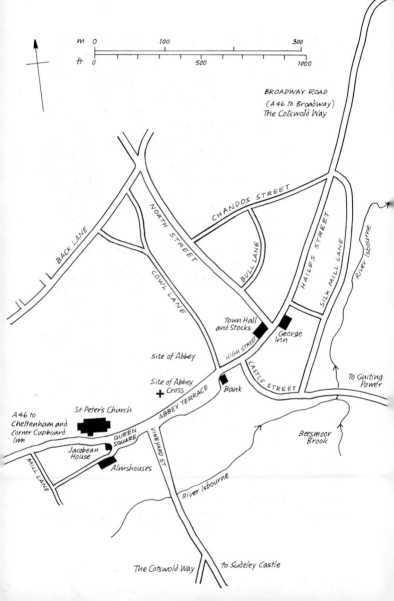

Winchcombe has a very ancient history. It was important much
more than a thousand years ago, as the nearby Belas Knap Long
Barrow and Wadfield Roman Villa show and, by the time the other
Cotswold towns along the Way were acquiring wealth and
notability, Winchcombe's period of greatness was over.

The name Winchcombe is derived from the Saxon 'Wincel Cumb',
the valley with a bend(?), and it was as a Saxon town that it
achieved fame. Offa, King of Mercia when that kingdom was at its
most powerful, is said to have built a nunnery in the valley around
790. When Offa died in 796, he was succeeded by his son Egrid, who
died suddenly in the same year and was succeeded by Kenulf.
Kenulf founded an abbey here, and the town grew up around it.

When Kenulf died in 819, he was succeeded by his son Kenelm,
whose age at his succession is commonly believed to have been 7,
though ages up to 24 have been mentioned. There was also a
daughter, Quendryth or Quendreda, an ambitious and unscrupulous
girl whose lover was Ascobert, the boy's tutor. Quendryth
persuaded Ascobert to kill her brother and, with this end in view,
Ascobert took Kenelm for a day's hunting in the Clent Hills. The
boy knew what Ascobert intended. At one point, waking from a
short sleep in the forest to find Ascobert digging a grave, he told
him that this was not the place for the deed. To prove his point, he
pushed an ash twig into the ground; it immediately burst into full
leaf and flower. Nevertheless, Ascobert, having taken Kenelm to
another part of the forest, cut off his head with a long knife, while
the boy was reciting a 'Te Deum'. At the instant of decapitation, a
white dove flew from Kenelm's head with a scroll in its beak and,
flying with it to Rome, deposited it at the feet of the Pope. The
scroll bore a message in Saxon which, when interpreted, read:

> In Clent cow-pasture under a thorn
> Of head bereft lies Kenelm, king-born.

Monks were sent from Winchcombe to recover the body from the
thorn tree under which it was buried, together with Ascobert's knife.

The appropriate tree was miraculously identified, either by a shaft of light which shone from Heaven to illuminate it, or by a white cow which guided the monks to the spot. As the body was taken from the grave to be reburied by the side of Kenulf in Winchcombe Abbey, a spring welled up from the grave.

Further springs gushed out wherever the body was laid down on the way to Winchcombe. The last halt was on Sudeley Hill – the route to Winchcombe from Worcester must have been a somewhat roundabout one – and at this spot a chapel was raised. The spring was known as St Kenelm's Well. The chapel was demolished in 1830, but its site is well known. As the body was being taken to its final resting-place, the procession passed Kenulf's palace, built at the same time as the Abbey and traditionally placed at the site of Lloyds Bank in Abbey Terrace. Quendryth came to the window and, as the body passed, her eyes fell out of their sockets to signify her guilt.

As with most legends, there may be an element of truth in the story of Kenelm. In 1815, excavations of the foundations of the Abbey church revealed two stone coffins – one containing the bones of a grown man, and the other those of a child, and a large knife. The coffins are presumed to be those of Kenulf and Kenelm, although proof is lacking. They are on view in Winchcombe Church.

Of the subsequent fate of Ascobert nothing is known. Quendryth became Abbess of Southminster, but history does not record whether or not she was blind.

Following Kenulf's death, Mercia declined in importance. The Danes sacked the Abbey in the middle of the 9c, and it was not restored until the late 10c under King Edgar. The re-establishment was largely the work of St Dunstan, though St Oswald and Ethelwold, both Bishops of Worcester, were involved. St Dunstan was currently Abbot of Glastonbury and, being in touch with Fleury, where the Benedictine revival started, set it up as a Benedictine house. It had joint patrons, St Kenelm being co-protector with the Blessed Virgin, who protected all Benedictine houses. The Abbey was destroyed again in 1151. The monks had permitted some of the poorer townspeople to build their timber-and-thatch cottages near the Abbey to gain some protection from attack.

Unfortunately one of the cottages caught fire and the fire spread to the Abbey. It was rebuilt this time in the Norman style.

The Abbey seems to have prospered greatly, aided not only by the presence of the shrine of St Kenelm, but also by the astuteness of the abbots. Its rise to wealth began with Abbot Robert, around 1200, who bought interests in existing Winchcombe houses, and land on which he built new ones. The houses were then let for 'satisfactory' rents. Under the subsequent abbot, Thomas, relations between the Abbey and town reached a low point. It is clear that throughout its history, or at least from 1150 onwards, the town had a somewhat ambivalent attitude towards the Abbey. It provided the main source of income, from the accommodation and entertaining of pilgrims, but it was also a grasping landlord. Under Abbot Thomas, the town vicar – Henry de Campden – vented the communal spleen by ringing the church bells loudly at times most guaranteed to disturb the monks in their observance of the canonical hours. The abbot reported the vicar's provocative behaviour to the Pope, Gregory IX, but although a commission was set up in 1231 to investigate the problem, no action was taken. The Abbey remained unpopular, and in 1346 a band of townspeople broke in, assaulting the monks and stealing some valuables. The provocative bell-ringing was repeated in 1399, and this time the Pope issued a decree that there was to be no ringing at night.

The last abbot but one was also the most famous – Richard Kidderminster. He was made abbot in 1488 at the age of 28, and remained in office for 37 years. He had a lasting association with Henry VIII which began when he preached before him, receiving a fee of 20 shillings. In 1512 he was made the King's ambassador to the Pope, and in 1521 he composed the official reply of the Church to the teachings of Martin Luther. He remained influential even after resigning as abbot in 1525, particularly so after signing the petition to Pope Clement requesting Henry VIII's release from his marriage to Katherine of Aragon. Since he was held in high regard by the Holy See, this act – in 1530 – increased the favour in which he was held by Henry VIII and Thomas Cromwell, who was a patron of Winchcombe Abbey. He remained a friend of Cromwell's until his death in 1531 at the age of 71. His death spared him from seeing his

friend Cromwell preside over the destruction of the Abbey he had
joined as a boy of 15 and served for 56 years.

The end came for Winchcombe 'on a cold and windy night',
23 December 1539, when the last abbot, Richard Anselm Mounslow,
and the last of the monks surrendered the Abbey and left. As usual
the plate went to the King, the Abbey itself being granted to Sir
John Bridges, and then to Lord Seymour of Sudeley. The roofs were
stripped of their lead and most of the buildings were destroyed. Of
the little that remained, the elements and the local townsfolk
searching for building stone took their toll. By 1714 the site was
levelled, and nothing of the Abbey could be seen. Today the site is
still unexcavated; it lies on private ground behind the high wall
opposite Abbey Terrace. A cross marks the position of the high
altar, the only monument to a religious life that lasted here for 700
years. It is said that the ghostly chanting of monks can still be heard
from the old site on still nights.

Evidence of the use of stone from the Abbey for other buildings
can occasionally be seen: in Court Lane, for instance, which was
close to the site, some of the old stones are marked with a 'W', the
quarry-mark for Winchcombe Abbey.

With the passing of the Abbey, Winchcombe suffered greatly. A
petition, supported by the Chandos family of Sudeley, was made to
Queen Elizabeth I in 1575 to help the town, which was in a state of
'ruin, decay and extreme poverty'. The Queen granted a charter for
two Saturday fairs, but this was hardly enough, and in 1640
Winchcombe was described as a 'poor, beggarly town'. Not long
afterwards, the town suffered further when the entire local area,
particularly Sudeley, was ravaged in the Civil War.

Between 1575 and 1640 Winchcombe had, however, enjoyed a
modest, but transient, prosperity based on the growing of tobacco.
This was first planted by one William Stratford, and the successful
result led to a rapid expansion of tobacco-growing towards
Cheltenham, with isolated fields as far away as Bristol. Eventually
the competition from the home-grown product forced the
government into taking action to protect the industry of the recently
created Virginian colonies. To ensure a monopoly for the colonies,
tobacco-growing was made illegal, and there were riots in the area

as government troops attempted to destroy the crops. On one occasion a mob attacked a company of soldiers who had been sent to destroy a field, killing both men and horses. The local resistance was of no avail in the long run, since the government was implacably on the side of the new colonies and, despite some illicit growing, the trade declined. It is interesting to note that as late as 1692, some 50 years later, a large plantation of illicit tobacco was destroyed near Bristol.

The presence of the Abbey in the town had effectively removed the incentive to attempt other business ventures. Most seriously, it appears to have prevented Winchcombe from gaining any benefit from the wool trade on which the other Cotswold towns flourished. Why is not certain, unless it was simply too easy to make a living off the pilgrims. It is often said that Benedictine monks were not 'agricultural', as were the Cistercians in Hailes, for instance, yet in the early 14c Winchcombe was one of only 12 religious houses in England and Scotland that could provide 40 sacks of wool per year. Under Richard Kidderminster, in particular, the Abbey had become notably learned, and this scholarly spirit may have had a local influence. Nevertheless there was a small clothing trade, a hoard of cloth being discovered in Sudeley Castle in the Civil War. One local who did well from the clothing trade was Jack Smallwood, 'Jack of Newbury', who made a fortune in Newbury after leaving the town. He was so rich that he raised, equipped and led a force of 300 men at the battle of Flodden Field. He is famous as the manufacturer of Winchcombe jerseys. Despite this, and one or two other doomed ventures, the town could offer little in the way of employment in the 18c and 19c. Silk Mill Lane commemorates, in name, one short-lived venture, the introduction of silk-throwing. The mill provided work for only about 30 adults but, in addition, for over 100 children. These children, all about 8 years old, were employed to change the bobbins and had to get up before 6 a.m. to do half a day's work before school. Near the mill was a tannery which also offered hard work for low wages, and further down the River Isbourne at Postlip there were two paper-mills, dating from the 18c, an industry which has survived to this day. The harshness of the working environment matched that of normal life. In 1800 two women were publicly flogged for hedge-pulling, and the stocks, still preserved, were in use as late as 1860 as a punishment for drunkenness. There was no water supply until the late 19c and the unmetalled streets were so muddy in winter as to be hardly passable.

This lack of latter-day prosperity is evident in Winchcombe's lack of an architectural 'wholeness', such as can be seen in Campden, and will be seen later in Painswick. Though the names Mill Street, North Street and Vineyard Street survive from the 13c, there are no buildings of that period. Vineyard Street was previously called Duck Street, not from the wildfowl on the rivers but from a ducking stool for witches and 'scolds'. The George Inn had the Norman name 'Le George' until the early 16c but was rebuilt by Richard Kidderminster in that century. It catered not only for pilgrims but also for the scholars who visited the Abbey because of its academic excellence. The initials 'R.K.' can be seen on the door to the

Winchcombe: The town stocks

Winchcombe: A worthy – one of the gargoyles of St Peter's church

courtyard. It is a galleried inn, and there is a legend that a Royalist soldier hiding from the Roundheads hid in the gallery but was discovered when the plume fell from his hat, and was taken outside the inn and shot. Opposite the George is the town hall, in front of which the old stocks are preserved. Here is the town museum that houses exhibits from Belas Knap and the Wadfield Roman Villa, together with items of local industry of later centuries. The town hall is on the site of a building of similar purpose that was built in the late 12c.

Another inn of great character is the Corner Cupboard on the corner of Mill Lane and Gloucester Street. This at one time belonged to the Merrett family, one of whom, Christopher, was an early Gloucestershire botanist who published a book entitled *Pinax* in 1666. This was one of the first records of English flora and fauna, and in addition contained the first known list of English birds. Opposite the inn is a house with a delightful string course of Tudor roses and hares. It is thought that the hares are a play on the name of the first owners.

Also interesting, architecturally, is Queen's Square, opposite St Peter's Church. Here is the Jacobean House, constructed in 1619 as King's School House, and attributed to Inigo Jones. The house was purchased by the Dent family of Sudeley in 1876 when it was in an advanced state of decay, and was renovated and renamed. Beside the house are the almshouses of Lady Dorothy Chandos, dated 1573. The Chandos family were lords of the manor, living in Sudeley Castle. The almshouses had 12 rooms for 12 old women, each of whom had her own garden and obtained water from a communal pump.

The church opposite was built in the Perpendicular style around 1470, though the site was an ancient one. The exterior of the church is of considerable interest. The belfry tower is 89 ft high and shows the marks of Roundhead shot. Nearer to the ground are the marks of bullets where Cavalier prisoners were lined up and shot. The tower is topped by a superb weathercock, by far the finest in the Cotswolds and one of the best in Britain. This massive bird originally sat on top of St Mary Redcliffe, Bristol. The other fine external feature is the array of 40 gargoyles, magnificent in their

ugliness. Look especially for the winged man in the top hat. Since it
was not unknown for the makers of gargoyles to caricature local
personages whom they disliked, the group is sometimes called the
'Winchcombe Worthies'. It may be, however, in view of the troubles
between the town and the Abbey, that the gargoyles represent
unpopular members of the monastic order.

Inside the church are numerous interesting relics. The two stone
coffins from the Abbey site have already been noted. Also from the
Abbey is a small oak door with the initials 'R.K.', another reminder
of Abbot Kidderminster. The almsbox has been in the church for
about 450 years. It was hollowed from a single tree and, following a
decree of Edward VI, has three locks so that it could be opened only
in the presence of the vicar and both church wardens.

The most interesting, and certainly the rarest, relic is the altar
cloth framed on the N wall. This frontal is a patchwork of two 14c

Winchcombe: The Corner Cupboard Inn

copes with a surrounding border containing pomegranates. The pomegranate was the emblem of Queen Katherine of Aragon and it has been suggested that this was the work of the Queen herself. The frontal was sent to the Royal School of Needlework for repair and while there, by a remarkable coincidence, was placed next to embroideries from Minsterworth, one of which was discovered to be the missing crucifixion panel from the centre. Unfortunately it was decided not to relocate the panel.

The elaborately carved organ case is reputedly the work of Grinling Gibbons, and the Tudor oak screen is also a masterpiece of carving. Particularly fine is the border of otters and foxes moving between bunches of grapes. An imp's head peers out from a boss near the pulpit. There is some original 15c glass in the S aisle windows, but the modern (1886) E window is also of considerable merit.

The church has no memorial brasses, but the tomb of Sir Thomas Williams is excellent. Sir Thomas, of Corndean, who died in 1636, is shown in full relief, kneeling in armour on one side of the tomb. He stares across to the recess left for a figure of his wife. Sadly, however, she remarried and is buried with her second husband, leaving Sir Thomas to kneel in lonely vigil for nearly 350 years.

Sudeley Castle

The Way continues down Vineyard Street, which is clearly marked as leading to Sudeley Castle. The entrance to the castle grounds is reached just beyond the bridge over the River Isbourne.

The history of Sudeley is closely allied to that of Winchcombe, the name being derived from its position, in the 'south clearing'. Its history, like that of Winchcombe, dates back to Saxon times, but there was no castle at that time, only an estate prized for its deer-hunting. At the time of the Norman Conquest, the estate was held by a great-grandson of King Ethelred the Unready. The first castle was built illegally during the wars between Stephen and Matilda, as were many others in that confused time. In the mid-14c it came into the hands of the Boteler family. The most famous of this line, Ralph, campaigned in France with Henry v and Henry vi, and could claim to have seen Joan of Arc die at the stake. Ralph was made

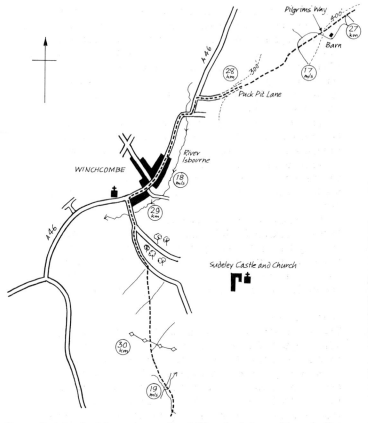

Baron Sudeley for his services as Lord Chamberlain, and he rebuilt
the castle, the resulting building being so magnificent that it aroused
both admiration and envy. Much of what remains today is Boteler's
work, including St Mary's Chapel, the banqueting hall, the tithe
barn and the Portmore Tower. The tower is believed to have been
named after a French admiral whose ransom, with other spoils of
war, helped finance the building. Ralph chose the wrong side in the

Wars of the Roses, and the castle was confiscated by Edward IV. It later had numerous owners who witnessed, at first hand, the founding of the Tudor dynasty. Katherine of Aragon stayed here, and Anne Boleyn spent a week here with Henry VIII, in their happier times. Each of these queens was to produce a daughter who remembered Sudeley. The third of Henry's queens, Jane Seymour, had a brother, Thomas Seymour, who became Lord Sudeley and lit the fuse for the spectacular Tudor drama enacted around the castle. In 1543 Thomas attempted to marry Katherine Parr, but was thwarted by her marriage to the King. Following Henry's death in 1547, Seymour, by then Lord High Admiral, did marry Katherine, the King's widow, intending to use her as a stepping-stone in his aim of becoming Lord Protector of the young Edward VI. He also tried to seduce the 15-year-old Princess Elizabeth who, at one time, lived at Sudeley with them. There is an interesting Gloucestershire legend

Sudeley Castle and gardens

Sudeley Castle: The remains of the banqueting hall

regarding this stay of Elizabeth's, it being said that she died at
Sudeley and that the scheming Seymour replaced her by a boy from
a local village. The legend persisted, being used to explain the
Queen's spinsterhood and masculine habits. But although the young
Princess did not in fact die, Katherine Parr did, of puerperal fever, a
week after the birth of Seymour's daughter Mary.

From writings of the time, it appears that Katherine was a kindly
and scholarly person. She was a convinced Protestant, and was
interested in the advanced religious theories of the day. Proof of this
lies in her appointment of Miles Coverdale as almoner. Coverdale
was continuing the work of William Tyndale, who will be met with
again further south, in translating the Bible into English.
Katherine's funeral service was actually conducted in English, a very
early example of outright Protestantism, the preacher being
Coverdale. Interestingly, the chief mourner was Lady Jane Grey,
Seymour's niece, suggesting that he was not present. Some have
interpreted this as proof of the speculation that Seymour had
poisoned his wife, but there is no evidence to support this.

Seymour eventually outreached himself and his attempt to
improve his position by marrying Lady Jane Grey to Edward VI
failed. He was executed, as was his niece, when Mary became
Queen. His lands, including Sudeley, were confiscated and of his
young daughter nothing more is known.

Queen Elizabeth visited the castle several times in her reign, and
Sudeley enjoyed a period of peace, which was destroyed by the Civil
War. By then the castle was in the hands of Lord Chandos, a
Royalist supporter. It was taken by Colonel Massie's Parliamentary
forces in early 1643 and used as a billet. During this time, the
soldiers looted the castle and desecrated the chapel. They tore down
Katherine Parr's tomb and threw her lead coffin into the gardens, a
Puritan gesture towards what they regarded as superstitious and
idolatrous customs. There were other acts of vandalism; an account
printed in 1685 speaks of the carcasses of slaughtered animals being
hung from the pulpit and the use of the altar as a chopping-board.
The nave was full of the entrails of butchered animals and the dug-
up bodies of the dead, and the far corners of the church were used
as makeshift toilets. These outrageous acts, whatever the muddled

thinking lying behind them, are hardly more than an instance of the mindless violence of soldiers and a comment on the horror of war generally.

The castle changed hands several times in the next two years. In 1643 King Charles stayed there following the raising of the siege of Gloucester, and wrote a letter to the County of Cornwall expressing his regret at the death of Sir Bevil Granville at the battle of Lansdown, a battlefield that the Way crosses further S. The letter is kept at the castle.

Finally Chandos surrendered to Parliament, paying a fine for the privilege of keeping his land, though he had to agree to the

Sudeley Castle: Katherine Parr's tomb in St Mary's Church

'slighting' of the castle, that is, to its being rendered useless for
military purposes. The castle was in a poor state after the war and
continued to decay, becoming an inn in the mid-18c. Later it was
used by tenant farmers, one of whom discovered Katherine Parr's
coffin in 1782. He opened it, and the body was found to be in a
near-perfect state of preservation. Over the succeeding years it was
opened often, and parts of the contents, including a large part of the
hair, were stolen for personal collections. Eventually, in 1817, the
body was at last reburied. Shortly after this, Sudeley was bought by
the Dent brothers, who restored the castle and chapel and erected a
marble tomb for the remains of Queen Katherine.

Sudeley Castle is still in the hands of the Dent family, who over
the last 150 years have contributed much to Winchcombe and the
surrounding area. The house and gardens have been extensively
renovated and now represent one of the best examples of the early
fortified mansion in the country.

The next section of the Way, to Humblebee Cottages, is a little difficult to follow, even with a map, and will be given in some detail. It leaves the road to the R some few hundred yards from the Sudeley Castle entrance, by a path signposted 'Humblebee 1¼ km, Belas Knap 2¼'. Go diagonally across the field, aiming at a distant telegraph pole, and cross a stile in a thicket hedge. Keep on towards the pole, on which, by now, a white marker is visible. Go over the stile next to the pole. Now head for the diagonally opposite corner, but before reaching it, take the (unmarked) bridge slightly L over the small stream at the field edge. Turn R and follow the hedge around L to a break in it. Go through and continue along the hedge again until Wadfield Farm comes into view. The farm is a beautifully elegant house, symmetrical about a superb doorway. Go round it on the L side.

During this section of the Way, and to the Humblebee Cottages, the scarp is again being ascended, giving good opportunities to pause and look back to Winchcombe and Sudeley, the town and castle finely situated in a glorious valley.

The Humblebee Cottages are interesting if only for the prosaic explanation of the name. 'Hamol hoh', 'scarred hill', has become Hamly, Humbly, and Humblebee. The final name conjures up pictures of fairy-tale cottages; the fantasies are better than the reality, although the little group does have a certain charm. To the R, hidden amongst a knot of fir trees, is the Wadfield Roman Villa. It is interesting that the Romans often chose villa sites that were set on the sides of hills, no doubt having an eye for a view. The villa is not well protected from the elements, or from the sheep, and has not been fully excavated. Around a small hut remains of walls at foundation level can still be seen. The hut itself is unlocked and contains the remains of a mosaic pavement about half complete. The hut, being unlocked, is also visited by the sheep in bad weather, which makes it necessary to clean your boots after a visit. It is none the less an interesting site, but is privately owned.

The Way now follows a well-signposted route to the Belas Knap Long Barrow, one of the highlights of the route.

Description of the route continues on p. 104.

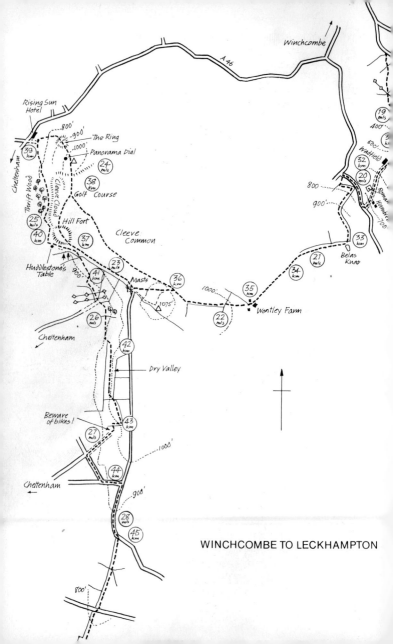

WINCHCOMBE TO LECKHAMPTON

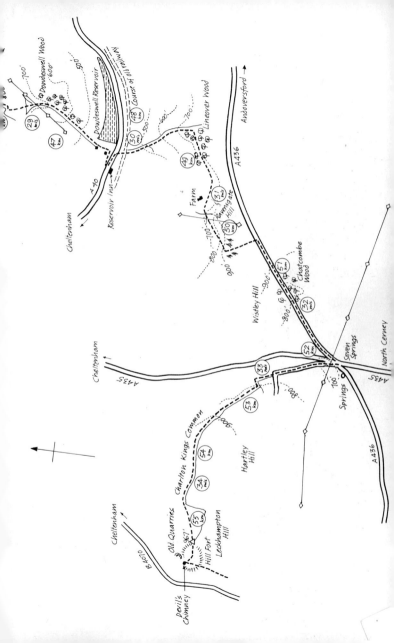

Belas Knap

Long barrows are the burial chambers of the Neolithic farming cultures, dated at between 4,000 and 3,000 BC. The barrows of the Severn Vale are so numerous and distinctive that they have been classified as a specific group, the Severn–Cotswold series. In that group three general forms are noted that probably represent the evolution of the structure. The first type, of which Hetty Pegler's Tump on the Way further S is a fine example, had an entrance leading to a passageway off which were one, two or three pairs of side-chambers or transepts. Next after this true-entrance phase came the false-entrance or false-portal phase, of which Belas Knap is, perhaps, the finest example. Here the entrance is blind, the burial chambers leading not off a passageway but directly into the mound from the sides. Again the chambers are in pairs. The final phase again had a false portal, but the chambers were randomly

The w chamber of Belas Knap long barrow

BELAS KNAP

distributed along the mound. Though Belas Knap is generally accepted as falling into phase two, it does in fact have an irregular pattern of chambers, there being no pairing of the SE chamber. The name Belas Knap is derived from 'bel', a beacon, and 'cnaepp', a hilltop, the present form having evolved from the 14c rendering, 'Belknap'.

In internal structure Belas Knap is similar to the others of the Severn–Cotswold series, in that the chambers are constructed of upright and roofing slabs of the local oolite. There may have been, in addition, some internal slab walls to assist the overall construction. Around the barrow is a low vertical dry-stone revetment or retaining wall, which is now mostly exposed but which was originally within the mound, the sloping rubble and earth cover of the mound continuing to the ground. The present mound is some 180 ft by 60 ft and $13\frac{1}{2}$ ft high at the highest point. Originally it must have measured 200 by 80 ft.

The false portal consists of a massive door-slab between two uprights with a lintel that was replaced in 1863 when early excavations broke the original. Behind the false door, the remains of an adult and five children were found. The 'horns' are convex and are of superb dry-stone walling, though only the lower sections are original, the upper sections having been restored during excavation work. It is believed that the horns enclosed an area that was used for ritual purposes during interments. Similar horns are found on the first-phase barrows, but the orientation of Belas Knap is N–S, not E–W like the earlier ones, so that the rituals themselves must have changed. Why the false-portal type replaced the true-portal is not known. It is generally assumed that it was an effort to defeat tomb robbers, although it may also have been a ritual practice to confuse evil spirits as to the true position of the dead.

The side chambers are reached by short passages of dry-stone walling. The NW and NE are five-sided, the SE chamber being rectangular. The paired chambers contained the remains of 26 burials, a further 4 being found in the single chamber. The southern chamber is something of a mystery: the present structure, which in appearance is a smaller version of the false portal, gives an incorrect impression in that the mound almost certainly covered it, possibly by means of a vanished roof-slab. The only slab found was the back-slab, there being no dry-stone passageway, either. The dry-stone revetment crossed what is now the entrance to the chamber, and it is believed that there was in fact no true chamber, although there may have been an internal cist, or stone-lined burial pit, at this point.

The finds from Belas Knap have been poor, but have included Roman coins and pottery, suggesting that there has been a long history of amateur excavations which may have led to the loss of any original burial ornaments. Today nothing remains on the site except the mound itself. Some of the remains are in Cheltenham Museum.

Before leaving, look again at the original dry-stone walling of the lower portal horns. It is identical to all the walling you have already seen, and will see on the route. The Cotsaller's art has lasted some 6,000 years – surely one of the most lasting of all art forms.

Belas Knap to Cleeve Common and Leckhampton

Leave Belas Knap alongside the wall running approximately W, and pick up the track down to Wontley Farm. Here another westerly track is followed that leads up to Cleeve Hill. Soon after the farm, as the wall to the L ends, the country changes. Cleeve Hill is the last unenclosed land in the high wolds and some of its bleak moorland character remains, though this is most evident here at the edge of the hill, near Wontley, since the hill itself has been taken over by a golf course and car park.

From the wall end there are two possible tracks. The one going straight on is marked as the principal Cotswold Way, with an arrow and dot, the path going L having a wooden marker post. You go L if you want to visit the highest point on the Wolds, straight on if you do not. The path L leads towards the radio masts. The highest point on the Cotswolds is marked by a trig point a few hundred yards SW of the masts. It is not obvious that this is the highest point of the broad plateau, and a slight feeling of disappointment about the lack of a true summit may be heightened by the cars parked along the wall on the Common itself.

Waymarkers at the masts point NW along the wall. You may see a waymarker arrow to the L pointing S: this indicates the route where it passes the northbound Way after this detour N to the Ring. Head for the fenced-off copse, to meet beyond it the alternative route coming directly from the wall end, near the edge of the Cleeve Hill Camp. There are many tracks on the hill, and one heads directly for its northern tip, but this misses the hill fort. This comprises a semicircle of man-made defences, the other half being formed by the natural cliff-line. The area enclosed is about 2 acres. The defences are a double rampart separated by a berm, or area of level ground. In the centre of the fort is one of the greens of the local golf course.

Leave the fort northward, with metal railings L. The railings bar the way on to Cleeve Cloud, a formation that is seen to better advantage later. The name is derived from 'clif', a cliff, and 'clud', a rock, or rock mass. The route northward offers fine views of Castle Rock, the turret-like mass, seen from above. Follow the path towards the high point of the hill in the general direction of the clearly marked 15th and 16th tees.

Below the trig point, a second ancient ditch is passed. This may have been the northern defence line of a projected, larger hill fort. Near the trig point is an elegant panorama dial pointing out the major features of the view, which is superb – down into the Winchcombe Valley and on to Broadway, and S to two points on the route, Leckhampton Hill and Painswick Beacon. Painswick is about half-way along the route, yet it looks close enough to touch on clear days.

Go NW and descend steeply, passing at one point a curious feature not, as yet, well understood. This is the Ring, a circular enclosure with bank and ditch some 30 yards in diameter. It is undoubtedly ancient, possibly a very early form of ritual circle preceding those made of upright stones. More recently it has been used as a green for the golf course.

Just below the Ring the track goes due W to emerge at the head of Rising Sun Lane, running down to the inn of that name and the A46. Here the Way turns to head S along a stony track that is a stream in winter. Along it can be seen superb views of Castle Rock and Cleeve Cloud to the L.

Care is needed on this section to keep on the right path. As Thrift Wood, to the R, ends, the Way goes L off the main track. Look for the waymarking arrows on stones. Eventually the radio masts come into view. As the track ends its level section and starts to climb to the hill above, there is an interesting feature R, a cuboid dressed stone known as Huddlestone's Table. This is named after Sir John Huddlestone, who was granted common rights on Cleeve Hill in the 16c, but the stone was ancient by then, reputedly marking the place where King Kenulf gave his speech of farewell to the guests who had attended the dedication of his Abbey at Winchcombe.

Now go up on to the hill, keeping to the wall on the R until the Common noticeboard and waymarkers are reached. The Way now descends, as you expect, but then surprisingly ascends again, reaching the 1,000-ft contour once more in a distinctive dry valley. It is now that the walker realises the true scale of the Common, and also the nature of the Cotswolds – not true hills, but a high plateau with a western scarp face and E–W valleys giving the impression of individual peaks. After the dry valley, the bleak country returns with a fine belt of gorse that is skirted to arrive at a modern cultural feature – hummocks of land used for motor-cycle scrambling. Risk all by crossing it direct, or go L and R to avoid it, and then follow the signs to Dowdeswell Reservoir. The route is straightforward, but passes a row of mutilated trees that look especially headless and hideous when leafless. The Way then enters Dowdeswell Wood and descends from the high Wold back into a valley.

The path through Dowdeswell Wood is a good introduction to the wood-walking of the central section of the Way. It is narrow and muddy in bad weather, but quiet and shady on summer evenings. There are occasional glimpses of the Dowdeswell Reservoir and the walker is tempted to linger. If it is evening, beware: the wood is said to be haunted by the ghost of a local man, one of the last to be hanged for sheep-stealing.

The Way emerges onto the A40 and goes E for a few yards before heading S again. In those few yards is the Reservoir Inn, where some walkers have been known to find comfort.

The Way heads S on the track signposted 'Seven Springs, Leckhampton Hill' that crosses the course of the old Great Western Railway line, long since stripped of rails. Soon it reaches Lineover Wood, named from 'Lind ofer', the lime-tree hill. Though small, this wood is very pleasant; few people visit it, and it remains unspoilt.

Dowdeswell Reservoir

On emerging from the wood, a waymarker post is seen in the middle of the field, and beyond it the steep scarp of Ravensgate Hill. The path ascends the hill diagonally, and the climb is perhaps the hardest on the route when travelling it from N to S. It is soon over, though, and a gentle track leads through the Wistley plantation and down to the main road. Turn R and follow the A436 to the crossroads outside Seven Springs.

The springs themselves are slightly off the route, a few yards down the A436 from the crossroads. It is sometimes said that this place is the true source of the River Thames, but it is generally agreed that it is in fact the source of the Churn, the Thames starting at Coates near Cirencester, north of Thames Head Bridge. The spot itself is well worth a visit, a small hollow surrounded by fine beech-trees.

The Way takes the minor road leaving the main A436 a few yards N of the crossroads and continues along this road and the track that leaves it as it swings W, to emerge on the side of Charlton Kings Common.

The climb to the top of the Common is superb, the track running through gorse bushes with excellent views, first of Cleeve Hill and Cheltenham, together with the valley to the R. Then, as the track bends around to the L, the Malverns come into view. There are also fine prospects of the scarp slope itself. The waymarking for the westerly traverse is poor; but keep high up and head for the trig point when it comes into view and there is no danger of straying from the route. From the summit there are views W to May Hill, the first of the Welsh Hills, Churchdown, Robins Wood Hill etc.

The trig point itself is near the ramparts of the Leckhampton Hill Fort, and represents the highest point of that hill, rather than of Charlton Kings Common, though the distinction is somewhat academic. Like Cleeve Hill Fort, the fort is a single semicircular rampart continuing with the natural scarp edge to form a defended area of some 6 acres. The name is derived from 'Leac ham Tun', a homestead where garlic is grown.

From the trig point, take the well-signposted path to the Devil's Chimney, a worthwhile, short detour. The Chimney is a remnant, as is the quarried scarp nearby, of the very extensive quarries that existed here until the early part of this century. It is probable that stone was quarried here from very ancient times because of the depth of the freestone, 100 ft in places. Certainly by the late 19c, the quarries on the Leckhampton edge were being worked extensively, and were so rich that an extensive system of tram- and railways had been produced to remove the stone. Some of the inclines were very steep, as much as 1 in 2. Eventually the mine owners overreached themselves. In 1922 it was claimed that over 78 million tons of stone were readily available, and that 272,250 tons could be produced annually for hundreds of years. The value of the workings was estimated to be £125,000. A new company was formed, and in October 1922, the Rt Hon. Dr McNamara, MP, Minister of Labour, came to cut the first turf. There was an immediate bad omen when the silver spade used bent beyond repair, and the turf had to be cut with an ordinary spade.

The venture was dogged by misfortune from the start. A waggon

Leckhampton Hill: The Devil's Chimney

containing 6 tons of material broke free from the horse hauling it and careered down one of the steeper inclines, causing considerable devastation at the bottom. Later a similar accident happened to an engine drawing ten loaded waggons. There were problems with the blasting, which not only weakened the building stone produced, but caused so much annoyance locally that the company was taken to court.

The quarry company eventually went into liquidation in October 1925, almost three years to the day from the bending of the silver spade.

The Devil's Chimney appears to be a remnant of those quarrying days. It is believed that an original smaller chimney was enlarged by the quarrymen during their operations, and acquired from them its present name, with a sprinkling of legend. Currently the Chimney is in grave danger of collapse, and it is unwise to climb it, though many have done so; the present record is said to be 13 people on the top at one time.

The Way continues around the Leckhampton Edge to the road and then skirts the Salterley Grange Sanatorium to emerge, after pleasant walking, in Ullenwood ('Owls' Wood'). Opposite the path (where it emerges on to a road) behind the wall is an ornamental pond belonging to Ullenwood Manor, a fine old mansion now used as a disabled youth training centre. Go R past the manor and down to the B4070, from which there is a good view to the Devil's Chimney. Cross the road and pass the eerily empty military camp to the L, reminiscent of the empty towns in old Western B movies.

The Shurdington Long Barrow comes into view L and shortly afterwards the Way goes L at a signpost marked 'Crickley Hill 1'. The barrow itself is neither on the route nor on a right of way, and is in a poor state of repair, though the remnants of horns are visible at the E end. Its best feature is its name, which also applies to a village to the NW. The derivation of the name is controversial; it could come from 'scerde', a pass or gap, though this is unlikely, as there is no such feature nearby; 'scryrd', cutting, as in harvest; or, from a possible nickname of a hypothetical owner, 'scydra', meaning hare-lipped.

Continuing to Short Wood, a name that accurately describes a short wood of magnificent and massive beech trees, we emerge on to Crickley Hill with its hill fort that is at once the best understood and, for that reason, the most disappointing of those on the route. The extensive excavations have had to be refilled so that only the description of the finds remains. The site itself is rather poorly defined, a situation that has not been improved by extensive quarrying of the NW corner, though this has not destroyed other large areas of the fort.

The remains of the Iron-Age rampart are visible, though the entrance, where many exciting finds were made, is difficult to locate except by those with a discerning eye for the recent spoil. The rampart of the inner Neolithic settlement is also visible.

The work of excavation is still being carried out by the Crickley Hill Trust, a charitable organisation, under the guidance of Dr Philip Dixon. Walkers who cross the hill in summer will probably

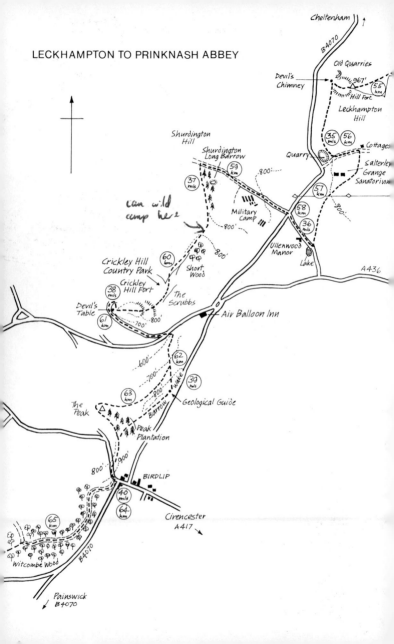

LECKHAMPTON TO PRINKNASH ABBEY

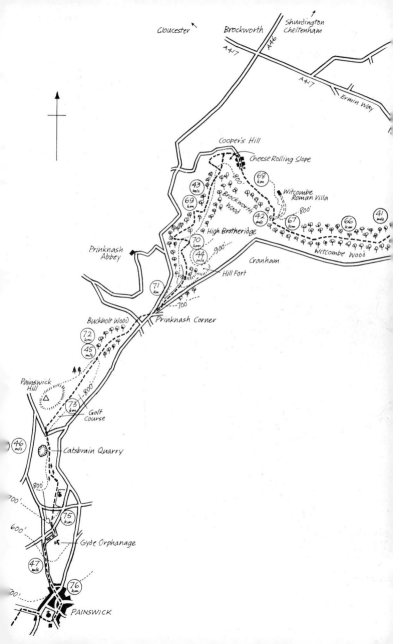

see the excavations in progress and can obtain a guided tour. Donations to the Trust are welcomed.

The work to date has shown that there were, in fact, three camps on the site. The first was Neolithic, dated at between 4,000 and 3,000 BC, and consisting of a single ditch and bank cutting off the hill promontory, the natural scarp slope forming the other defence. The defences were reconstructed several times and, at their most developed stage, the bank was faced with dry-stone walling and fenced on top.

After this early camp, the hill was deserted for a considerable period until, around 600 BC, the first Iron-Age camp was completed. This was larger than the earlier one, covering some 9 acres and containing houses for a considerable number of people, together with livestock pens and sheds. The ditch was 6 ft deep and the rampart 10 ft high with a fenced walkway. The entrance was a

Beeches in Short Wood, Crickley Hill

straightforward double-gated arrangement, the gates separated by a narrow passageway. It appears that this fort lasted only 30–50 years and was then destroyed by burning.

Following a short period of desertion, a third camp was set up on the ruins, probably by reconstruction of the walls of the second camp, which had not been totally destroyed. A new entrance was built, of remarkable design. It was large and circular, with high walls topped by fenced walkways all round. A gated doorway led into the walled circle and a second led through the rampart itself. This, as was the usual practice, made an invader turn left between staggered entrances, so exposing his unshielded right side to the defenders, though the totally surrounded inner circle made this a less important aid to the defenders. This third camp, which contained an array of the roundhouses so recently made famous, also lasted only a short time and was again destroyed by fire, presumably as the result of an attack.

The next landmark on the route is the Devil's Table, another natural feature endowed with a sinister name for no apparent reason. This Table is, however, excellent as an eating-place, with fine views eastward.

Below the Table, the lane is followed to the main road and across it the Way continues up Barrow Wake. The official route does not take in the last steep section of the hill, traversing SW below it, but this misses the summit memorial to Peter Hopkins, 'Geologist and Christian, 1932–1966', on which is displayed, not the usual panorama, but the geology of some local and some more distant places – May Hill, the Malverns, Cleeve, Leckhampton, Crickley. It is a simple yet striking piece of work.

Those who have gone to the summit need not retrace their steps. Instead, go along the scarp edge, cross a field, and follow the track going slightly to the L through the wood until it meets, at right-angles, a more clearly-marked path. This path is the official Way which is reached by following the scarp around a few hundred feet below the Edge and coming over 'The Peak' to enter the wood. Follow the path to the road and go up it steeply to Birdlip.

The derivation of the name is a matter of debate. It could be from 'Bridd Hlep', 'bird's leap' because of its steepness, or 'Bryd Hlep', 'bride's leap', perhaps from an ancient tradition. However, 'Brid' might be a man's name, and 'hlyp' not a 'leap' but an 'enclosed space'.

The village is famous for the discovery of one of only two Iron-Age mirrors ever found. It is thought that the mirror and other jewellery belonged to a queen of the Dobunni who ruled from here just before the Romans came.

At the top of the hill go R on the B4070 and almost immediately R again on a track, signposted 'Cooper's Hill 4km, Prinknash 7km', that enters the Witcombe estate. Here is some of the finest wood-walking on the Way, through the quiet wood of 'Wid Cumb', the wide valley.

The Way is easily followed. It turns L off the easy track on to a less easy one at the sign 'To Keepers' Cottages', but is always well signposted. The wood is mature, without the profusion of impenetrable low scrub that occasionally spoils beech woods. At an obvious 180° bend, which has a spring on the R to supply a very pleasant drink, the track splits. The Way goes L, uphill, while the track to the R, downhill, leads to the Witcombe Roman villa. The villa is beautifully sited, though the builder had problems with the numerous springs on the scarp slope behind that threatened to undermine the entire structure. It is in the care of the DOE, though it is not always open to the public because of continuing excavation. The foundations are visible, and parts of the well-preserved bath-house are contained in huts. The mosaics of these rooms are unusual, showing seascapes with dolphins and fish.

The Way leaves the Witcombe Estate and wood near a superb Cotswold cottage, and immediately the view opens up, both backwards to the valley that has just been traversed, and ahead to Cheltenham and Cleeve. Continuing along it, we come to the base of the famous cheese-rolling slope of Cooper's Hill.

The origins of cheese-rolling are lost in antiquity. It is known that similar events took place elsewhere, for instance at the Uffington site, where there are springs at the bottom of the slope, as at Cooper's Hill. On the hill above Uffington is the famous White Horse carving, and it is interesting that another famous carving, the Cerne Abbas Giant, is also on a slope at the bottom of which there were springs. At some of these places a wheel was rolled and, at one at least, a flaming wheel, so it is likely that the rolled object symbolised the sun. The ceremony originally took place at midsummer, when the days began to shorten to winter, so it is likely that the origin is a pagan one, intended to arrest the fading sun and ensure its return the following year. The Cooper's Hill festival is now held at the Spring Holiday; the contestants chase 7-lb cheeses down the 200-yard, 1-in-1 slope, the winner keeping the cheese.

In the past, the programme was more extensive. At one 19c festival the events included:

> 2 cheeses to be ron for
> 1 plain cake to be green for
> 1 plain cake to be jumpt in the bag for
> Horings to be dipt in the toob for
> Set of ribbons to be danced for
> Shimey to be ron for
> Belt to be rosled for
> A bladder of snuff to be chatred for by hold wimming

The first item is the traditional cheese-rolling; the second is face-pulling (grinning) through a horse-collar, still a feature of similar festivals in the Lake District; the third is a mystery, perhaps more hilarious for being so; the fourth is dipping for oranges in a tub; the fifth and seventh were dancing and wrestling for the ribbons and belt worn by the master of ceremonies, and still worn by him to this day; the sixth is a girls' race for a chemise; and the last involves old women talking loudly or long for the reward of a bag of snuff.

The former ceremony also included maypole dancing, but the current maypole is too close to the slope edge for that.

At the time of going to press, the slope has been temporarily fenced off to avoid erosion. But the view down the slope from the maypole is awesome.

The route from here goes through Brockworth Wood, which has a network of nature trails. Several boards are passed giving interesting information on the local plant life. The wood is being extensively cleared, and the (relatively) poor waymarking may lead the walker astray on to the lumber-roads, deeply rutted and difficult to pass. As a general rule, those who miss one of the waymarkers on the trees should keep to the western wood edge and head SE. In the late spring this section is notable for the overpowering garlic smell of ramsoms, or wood garlic.

The Way now ascends High Brotheridge, the high, broad ridge separating Witcombe and Cranham, by a steep climb, and descends into Buckholt Wood. On the descent a discerning eye can pick out the rampart of another Iron-Age camp.

Follow the minor road, when it is reached, down to Prinknash Corner. To the R from here is Prinknash (pronounced 'Prinage') Abbey, famous for its pottery, and also for the modern Abbey built quite recently with 2,500 tons of Guiting stone. It has bold, yet

Prinknash Abbey

simple lines. The Abbey is Benedictine, and replaces the monastery set up in 1928 by the monks from Caldy Island in the original Prinknash manor house. The manor house was originally used by the abbots of Gloucester but passed into lay hands following the Dissolution. It was bequeathed to the Caldy Benedictines by Lord Rothes, the Benedictines passing Caldy on to the Cistercians.

The Way crosses the A46 and continues again through Buckholt Wood. Beyond it is Painswick Beacon.

Painswick itself, about half-way along the route, is a high spot in terms of the charm and beauty of Cotswold architecture. The surrounding area with its wooded valleys and springs offers an abundance of delightful walking. Nearby is a village perhaps aptly named Paradise.

Painswick Beacon – marked 'hill' on the maps – is a curious place. In 1907 it was described as a wonder to behold, because of the hill fort, but it is now difficult to envisage the site as it was then because of the golf-course and trackways. The hill is known also as Kimsbury Hill, The Castles and Castle Godwin. The first of these names, from 'Kynener's Burgh', is probably the earliest, but the last is historically the most interesting; it has been passed on to a house near Paradise.

Godwin was a great Saxon leader and Earl of Wessex whose daughter, Eadgyth, was married to Edward the Confessor, and whose son was Edward's successor, King Harold. In 1052 there was a disagreement between Godwin and the other great Saxon lord, Leofric, Earl of Mercia. To settle the quarrel Godwin marched his army towards that of Leofric, hoping to take Robin's Wood Hill prior to a final engagement. Unfortunately the hill was already held by King Edward, who had sided with Leofric, so Godwin camped on Painswick Hill. The civil war that threatened was averted by compromise, and in 1053 Godwin died. Some believe that it was this encampment of Godwin's army that gave the hill its name, though there is no evidence for a castle as such. Others believe that the name was added long afterwards and is not connected with Earl Godwin at all.

The Way crosses the hill below the high ridge with its trig point on the summit, but the diversion is worth while, even though the view is a little limited and in summer, particularly at weekends, the hill is popular with trippers.

Crossing the hill, go L (E) of Catsbrain Quarry into an interesting piece of conifer woodland. At its end go R (W) of the walled churchyard and down to the road. Turn L and enter Painswick.

Description of route continues on p. 138.

Painswick has rightly been described as the jewel of the Cotswolds, and on the Way it comes midway in the necklace of the Cotswold Edge. The distinctive, grey local stone gives it a somewhat sombre appearance, and the houses, which open on to the roads and pavements rather than standing back behind gardens, a certain formality. But for all that it is the most natural of the Cotswold towns and the most peaceful. It has not been abused by the needs of tourists and their cars, and those who have sampled the delights of its side streets as they should be sampled – on foot – hope it never will be.

The name is derived from two sources at two widely separated times. Wick is from the Saxon 'wicke', a village, though Alfred Watkins had a different theory. Watkins believed that the whole of Britain was criss-crossed with a system of ancient trackways that ran in dead straight lines – the ley lines. Many of these he believed were used to carry salt, that most important of substances, and he also believed that 'wick' denoted a salt way, deriving from the same root as white, the colour of salt. An example of his theory was Droitwich, from which several salt ways began. Certainly in the Cotswolds there are both White Ways and Salt Ways, and some believe they are interchangeable. The road from Painswick to Stroud is called Wick Street, though, of course, either explanation can be used to account for this name. Those interested in this and other ideas of Watkins' are referred to his book *The Old Straight Track*, published in 1925.

All sources are agreed that 'Pain' was appended around the mid-12c, Pain being the lord of the manor, Pain Fitzjohn.

Fitzjohn was one of the earlier lords of the manor, who, as a group, were remarkable, both for their status in history and for the violent manner of their deaths. Four were killed in battle, and two executed; one was murdered, one committed suicide; one fell off a ladder, and one had a wall collapse on him. Perhaps the most remarkable of all was the one who endured imprisonment in the Tower and died of joy when he was told he was to be released.

In Domesday Book, Roger de Lacy is named as lord of the manor

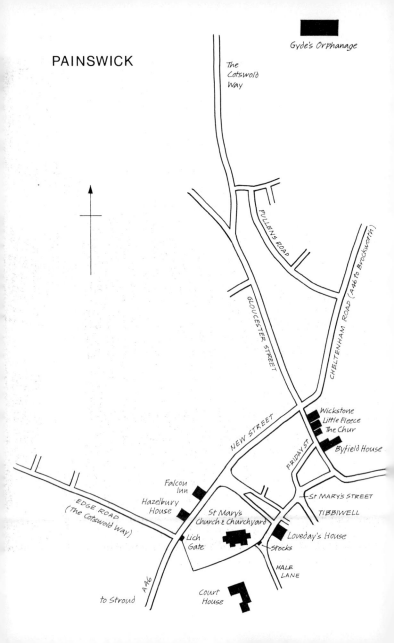

Painswick: The Post Office, a 15c timber frame house

that contained Wicke, which was also written Wyke and Wykeham. Roger was the son of Walter de Lacy, who had fought at Hastings with William the Conqueror, for which he was granted extensive land in Gloucestershire. Pain Fitzjohn acquired the manor by marrying the daughter of Hugh, Roger's brother, in 1130. From Fitzjohn, the manor passed to the de Munchersi family and then to the Talbots, who made a substantial contribution to the tradition of violent death. Perhaps the most famous was John, Lord Talbot, first Earl of Shrewsbury, whose place in history is assured for all time by his appearance in Shakespeare's *Henry VI, Part One*. Talbot had been Governor and Lieutenant of France under Henry VI, and Act IV, Scenes vi and vii of the play record his death and that of his son at the hands of the French. Members of the Talbot family also fought against the Berkeleys at the battle of Nibley Green, of which more will be said when the route reaches Nibley itself. At the battle Lord John Talbot's grandson, Lord Lisle, was killed.

When the Talbot line ended, the manor passed into the hands of Thomas Cromwell. Cromwell is most remembered as the principal agent in the dissolution of the great abbeys, but to reject him out of hand as a destroyer does him little justice. In fact he was a remarkable man, who rose to be Chancellor of England from humble beginnings as the son of a blacksmith. The ruthlessness and scheming he showed as Chancellor were a reflection both on the times and on the qualities which had allowed him to climb so high. Such qualities, however, are guaranteed to win few friends, and when his fall came he was executed, as so many had been who crossed his path in his days of power. While in the Tower awaiting his fate, Cromwell negotiated the sale of the manor with Sir William Kingston. The deal did not go through, because Cromwell's lands were confiscated, but Kingston was a favourite of Henry VIII and prevailed upon him to grant him the manor. On Sir William's death the manor passed to his son Sir Anthony, a man for whom the infliction of suffering seems to have been a delight, having a gift for cruelty unusual even by the standards of the day. He learnt to exercise this talent when he led a force of Gloucestershire men to suppress the northern rebellion, the Pilgrimage of Grace, following the 1536 Suppression Act that began the dissolution of the monasteries. By 1549 he was at the peak of his ability. In that year he was Provost-Marshal of the King's army that suppressed the western rebellion in Cornwall. The mayor of Bodmin had sided with the rebels but, following their defeat, pleaded that he had acted under duress and was in reality a loyal servant of the crown. His pleadings appeared to have won the day, and he was much relieved when Kingston invited himself to dinner with him, believing that Kingston could only be offering friendship. Consequently the mayor prepared an excellent feast and welcomed Kingston with open arms. Before the meal, Kingston called the mayor aside and told him that there were rebels in Bodmin, and that there must be deaths also. He asked that the mayor should have a gallows erected in the town with haste, to be ready by the end of the meal. The mayor, eager to comply with the wishes of so important a man, gave the order straight away, and host and guest sat down to eat. At the end of the meal, Kingston asked to be taken to the gallows and, on seeing it, queried whether it was strong enough. The mayor assured him that it was. On this, Kingston revealed that the gallows was provided for the mayor, who was thereupon hanged.

Later in 1549, the Enclosures Commission was arousing strong feelings in the neighbourhood of Painswick, and there had been riots and the destruction of fences. Kingston met this threat to the established order in his normal direct manner – he opened a prison in Painswick and had a gallows erected on nearby Sheepscombe Green. He granted three pieces of land for the upkeep of the gallows, the profits from the land being used for the preservation of the gallows itself, the ladders, and the halters for the condemned man. In addition he installed two men in a nearby house to act as executioners. In the 18c there was a piece of land in this area called Hangman's Acre, and in Laurie Lee's book *Cider with Rosie*, which is set in the area, there is a Hangman's House.

Kingston met a violent death which seems to match his life style. In the reign of Queen Mary his part in a plot to overthrow the Queen and install Elizabeth on the throne was discovered. He was captured and taken towards Coberley Court for trial. On the way there, at Lechlade, he was drowned while crossing the Thames with his escort. It has never been established whether his death occurred during a bid to escape or whether he committed suicide.

Following Kingston's death Painswick had a period of tranquility broken in 1643 by the Civil War. The Cotswolds played an important part in the Civil War, many of the towns on the Way being involved in one way or another. The reasons appear to be twofold: first, it was important to the King to control the area because it provided a background to his headquarters at Oxford, and a corridor from there to South Wales, which was one of his loyal areas; and secondly because its clothing trade was one of the most important sections of the economy. The King had to fight for possession of the area, since the clothiers were staunchly Parliamentarian; that is, the towns of Cirencester and Gloucester were for Parliament, but it is sometimes difficult to assess objectively the true sympathies of their leading inhabitants, since the towns were garrisoned by Parliamentary forces from an early stage of the conflict. The lesser towns probably bent with the wind, supporting the side whose troops were closest at the time.

In July 1643 the King's forces took Bristol and moved north to attack Gloucester. The King spent a night at Berkeley Castle and then another in Painswick, staying, most probably, in the Court House. From there he issued, on 10 August, a proclamation from 'our court at Payneswicke'. The proclamation was to the effect that any soldier found guilty of stealing or looting from any property possessed by the army would be executed. The King moved on to Gloucester and laid siege to it, a siege that he lifted on 8 September, realising perhaps – but too late – his mistake in not having marched to London. The King was back at Painswick again, on or around 10 September. There is a local legend that on this occasion, when one of the young royal princes asked his father when they were going home, the King replied that they had no home to go to, but this appears improbable, since the King's position at that time was by no means desperate.

Painswick escaped any real fighting at that time, but in 1646 a group of plundering Royalists attacked the town and its 'guard' of Parliamentarians. The guard, housed in or near the church, was heavily defeated, the death toll being about 50 with about 200 more imprisoned, initially in the church itself. The church itself was

damaged both by cannonballs and by fire, and marks of the attack
can be seen today on the tower and on the E and W walls.

By the time of the Civil War, Painswick was well established in
the Cotswold wool trade. The factors that made the Cotswolds in
general such a classic wool area, including the soil, and the breed of
sheep, were reinforced here by the excellence of the water supply in
the Slad valley leading down to Stroud, and by the woad, for
dyeing, which grew in the Painswick locality. Woad is now one of
the rarer of local flowers, although specimens can still occasionally be
found: a tall plant with clusters of small yellow flowers. It was not
the flowers that were used in the dyeing process but the blue-grey
leaves, from which was produced a dye for making blue, green and
black cloth. The leaves were ground to a pulp for this purpose, an
unpleasant job, since the smell given off in the process was, by all
accounts, indescribable.

The manufacture of woollen cloth was in evidence in Painswick
by the mid-15c. It was essentially a cottage industry. The rough
wool from the shearers was first sorted to remove burrs and other
impurities, and then scoured to loosen the natural greases. This
scouring was usually undertaken by boiling, sometimes in water to
which stale wine had been added. Following this, the wool was
rinsed in clean water and dried. It was then teased out on the
scribbling machines to give a more even and finer consistency, and
was then carded. Then came spinning, a difficult job that required a
high degree of skill from the wheel operators. Consistency was
demanded and, if it was not achieved, the wool was chopped up,
remixed and sent back to the spinner. It was usual for the spinner to
be paid only for accepted wool. The final processes were carried out
at the mill. First there was the fulling mill where the wool, having
first been beaten to make it more compact, was cleaned with fuller's
earth and then dressed up on the teasel frames. The teasels, set in
drums, raised the nap of the wool. The next job was shearing, when
the long, teaseled nap was hand-sheared to length. This job was
extremely skilled and called also for great strength, as the shears
were very heavy. Weaving was also done at the mill, by a master
weaver with assistants to set up the loom. Dyeing, carried out either
on the wool or on the cloth, was itself a skilled task. The dyeing of

the 'woaded colours' was usually done by a craft dyer specialising in this craft, as was the dyeing of scarlet. It was believed that the water in the Stroud area had a 'peculiar quality' which made possible the manufacture of an excellent scarlet cloth, and it is certainly true that the British army was clad in this scarlet. It is interesting, as you walk through the streets of Painswick, to remember that the thin red line of history was clad in the cloth manufactured in the mills of this small town, just as some of its wearers were the sons of the weavers who made it.

Fortunes were made from wool in the Cotswolds in general, and around Stroud in particular. But such fortunes were not made by the parters, who sorted it; the scourers, who scoured it; the brayers, who cleaned it; the burlers, who removed burrs; the carders, and the fullers; the rowers with their teasels; the weavers and the shearmen; the dyers, and the drawers who hid weaving faults by drawing loose threads together. For them it was unremitting toil for 14 hours a day, by candlelight in winter. The rewards were pitifully small and the housing, in general, poor. A census in 1608 showed that nearly a third of all male workers in the Painswick area were employed in one aspect or another of the wool trade.

But by 1700 the bubble was bursting. The 1678 'Burial in Woollen' Act referred to in the Introduction was a clutch at a vanishing straw. The export boom was over, and the shock waves hit the Cotswolds hard. The population of Painswick declined steadily from 1700 to 1850. In the earlier years of that period the trade was still good, though diminishing. The true cultural shock came in the mid to late 18c with the introduction of mechanisation: the spinning jenny of Hargreaves in 1764, the power loom of Cartwright in 1785 and, following these, the general use of steam-powered mills. The Cotswold mill owners were slow to realise the potential of these machines and the workers quick to oppose them, and consequently there was a shift in the centre of the cloth trade to the North where, despite opposition, mechanisation went ahead. The loss of trade of the local clothiers had an immediate effect on the local people, who were paid less for their work so that the profits could remain the same. The inequality of the rewards of mill owner and worker had long been a source of discontent, and reduction in wages was not a new development. In 1756 the weavers complained that the wages had been reduced to such an extent that the men could not earn sixpence a week even by working 16 hours on all 7 days. Not satisfied with the assurance of the owners, the men went on strike, and there were riots in Stroud, some of the owners being temporarily imprisoned in a meeting they were holding. Since strikes were at that time illegal, the government had to act quickly and troops were despatched to the area. The troops were led by a young colonel gaining his first experience of full command, a man later to be a famous general – James Wolfe.

The riots were suppressed, but the situation did not improve for the workers. The industry itself was dying, and by the early 19c it was all but dead. To squeeze out the last of the available profits, the owners resorted to child labour, with 9-year-olds working a 13-hour day. It is an interesting sidelight on the state of the country at that period that, in his speech moving the second reading of the Factories Regulation Act in 1832, Sadler said: 'You have limited the labour of a robust negro to 9 hours, but when I propose that the labour of the young white slaves shall not exceed 10 the proposition is deemed extravagant.'

In the Stroud area the poverty was appalling. There had been an old saying in Painswick that the inhabitants were too poor to live, yet too healthy to die, but this was no longer true. Whole families died, and the only remedy was to leave. Some went to the mines of South Wales and the Forest of Dean, others to the new worlds of Australia and America. A way of life was over.

At the height of Painswick's importance there were 25 mills on the streams from Cranham and Bull's Cross to Stroud, and the wealth from those mills built the fine houses and the church that we see today. The wealth was made out of human misery, but that is not the fault of the buildings, only of the owners. The buildings remain as a monument to the craft of the stonemasons and the builders.

Entering Painswick, the Way passes on the L Gyde's Orphanage, built with money bequeathed by Edwin Gyde, a local businessman who died in 1894. Where the main road goes L the walker carries straight on down Gloucester Street. At the crossroads the route is

straight across and down Bisley Street, and there the beauty of
Painswick starts in earnest. To the L are buildings which date from
the 14c. The first two, Wickstone and Little Fleece, are the remains
of the Fleece Inn. The arch over the ground floor window of
Wickstone was at one time the packhorse entrance to the courtyard
at the back of the inn. The cellars are reputedly haunted by a former
owner searching endlessly for treasure buried there. Next to Little
Fleece is the Chur, which also dates from the 14c and was once a
coffee house. Opposite Friday Street on the R, named probably
from the markets held there on Fridays, is Byfield House, which is
Tudor with a later frontage.

Continue to the end of Bisley Street and then turn R into
St Mary's Street. After Victoria Street has entered on the R there is,
to the L, a splendid example of an 18c Cotswold house. The house was
built for one of the Lovedays, who were among the older Painswick
clothing families, commemorated by tombs in the churchyard from
the early 17c right through until the late 19c, by which time the
family had become famous. The house is now the vicarage. At the
end of the street is the Court House, a magnificent early 17c
mansion with elegant tall chimneys and gables. The house stands on
the site of an earlier one which was pulled down in the mid-16c. The
present house, started in 1600, was built for Thomas Gardner, a
clothier. The Gardners were another old-established Painswick
family, the oldest tomb in the church being of one of the family.
Thomas did not keep the house for long, selling it to Dr John
Seaman, Chancellor of the Diocese of Gloucester, who added the
three-storey extension, on the first floor of which was the Court
Room itself. Dr Seaman died in 1623.

Now turn R to enter the churchyard, but before doing so note the
iron stocks to the R of the entrance. These were leg irons and there
is a hard stone seat behind them. It is believed that these irons,
which were uncomfortable for the wearer because of chafing, are
unique in Britain.

Beyond the stocks is St Mary's Church, the high spot of any walk
around Painswick, and arguably the finest of all Cotswold churches.
Painswick had a church as early as 1086, since Domesday Book
notes that Wyke had a priest. Very little remains of this early

Norman church, although it is reasonable to suppose that it was on the same site as the present one. The church has had a long history of building. St Peter's Chapel, N of the chancel, is believed to date from the late 14c. In the N aisle leading to it are two corbels which are believed to be of King Richard II and his Queen, Anne of Bohemia, dated around 1380. The tower was built in 1430, the spire being added in 1682. The S aisle was built in 1741 and rebuilt in 1877, and the S porch was added as late as 1969.

The tower and spire have an overall height of 174 ft, an impressive monument to the pride of the inhabitants of the town. One Sunday in June 1883, the spire was struck by lightning during a storm, and the upper 30 ft collapsed, some of the masonry falling through the belfry ceiling and some through the roof of the nave. Some of the tombs in the churchyard were also damaged. It was not possible to rebuild the top section because of potential damage to the lower, so the entire spire was demolished stone by stone so that it could be rebuilt in as near perfect a manner as could be managed. The rebuilding was carried out quickly at a total cost of £1,498 18s. 4d., collected from insurance and subscription, and the church was reopened within 6 months. The money raised more than paid for the damage, and the excess was used to install the carved oak choir stalls. The tower contains a peal of 12 bells, one of only about 30 in England and one of the most famous. Most of the bells are of an early period, the ringers' society, the quaintly named Ancient Society of Painswick Youths, having been formed in 1686, but the peal was increased from 10 to 12 in 1821. It is likely that this was in response to the increase in the Stroud church peal from 6 to 10, rivalry between 'Proud' Painswick and 'Strutting' Stroud being notorious throughout the days of prosperity for their towns.

The interior of the church is exquisite, a marvellous mixture of the best of the old and new, and not overburdened with obtrusive memorials. Above the pine pews and the applewood lectern is a superb vaulted ceiling, and beyond in the chancel a fine painted ceiling. The model ship represents an early symbol of the Christian Church, the Church being seen as a ship sailing through the high seas of all perils. Indeed the word 'nave' derives from the Latin *navis*, a ship. The actual ship represented is Sir Francis Drake's flagship *Bonaventure* which saw action in the defeat of the Armada. The model was made in the late 19c.

The church was badly damaged in the Civil War engagement in 1644, as has been mentioned. In addition to the marks on the exterior, the interior was badly damaged by fire started by 'grenadoes', an early form of hand-grenade. One of the items lost was the original font, the present one being a replacement dated 1661 and inscribed with the initials of the churchwardens of that time.

The stone cone next to the Victorian pulpit is the spire top replaced during repairs in 1950.

The only ornate tomb in the church is in the oldest part, St Peter's Chapel, and it is as interesting as it is unusual. It has been used by three separate families, the first being that of Viscount Lisle in 1356. The second was Sir William Kingston's in 1540, and the third the Seaman family in 1621. The alabaster effigies are of Dr John Seaman and his wife who had lived at the Court House. Between the effigies is a pile of law books looking like a working desk. The tomb was reconstructed after being badly damaged in the Civil War action when, it has been suggested, the local people damaged it in memory of Anthony Kingston. The damage could just as easily have occurred during the fighting or after, when the Parliamentarian prisoners were held in the gutted church. The far L nave pillar is inscribed 'Be bolde, be bolde, but not too bold', and this inscription is believed to have been carved at the same time.

The only other memorial of serious note is the one in the sanctuary to the Rev. J. Moseley, 'The Christian! The Scholar!! The Gentleman!!!'

The churchyard is as interesting as the church itself, containing probably the finest collection of carved tombs of any Cotswold church, and also the famous yew trees. The tombs are such an interesting feature that two pamphlets are available describing 'Tomb Trails', giving details of the interesting aspects of each. The trails are well worth following, but those with insufficient time should not miss the skeleton on that of Richard Poole, 1707, NE of the church; that of Jeremiah Caudwell, 1747, to the NW; and the winged skull on that of Edward Palling to the W. A very good group of tombs are those of the Poole family N of the church.

Many of the tombs were the work of the Bryans, a family of masons. The tomb of John Bryan (1716–1787), is the plain stone pyramid to the L of the main path to the lych-gate. Some say that the pyramid is a miniature of the Caius Cestius tomb in Rome, but it could equally be a comment on the elaborate tombs of his clients. To the R of the path near the lych-gate is the tomb of Thomas Hamlett, 1783, who was also a Freemason. His masons' tools are carved on the stone.

Yew trees are usually associated with churchyards, although the reason for the association is not well understood. It could be to protect the church and its inhabitants by offering a poisonous barrier to evil spirits; to represent, by its berries, the blood of the Passion; or to provide wood for longbows. The churchyard was chosen to plant them, it is said, because the farmers refused to allow the poisonous tree to be planted anywhere where cows might reach it. It

Painswick: Table tombs and yews in St Mary's churchyard

is interesting that despite its known poisonous effect yew juice was used as a cure for worms.

According to legend there are only 99 trees in the churchyard, and if a hundredth is planted one of them dies to maintain the same number. In fact there are over 100 now, pruned to form archways over the main paths.

The church is the scene of a curious ceremony on 19 September or the first Sunday following it, when it is circled by local children who sing hymns and dance round it. This service, known as the clipping ceremony, coincides with clipping of the yews, but this is likely to be a modern coincidence. In fact clipping is derived from the Saxon 'ycleping' – encircling or embracing – and when the ceremony took place first in 1897 it was probably the revival of an ancient one rather than an innovation. The ceremony is not unique to Painswick, though the timing suggests a very early pagan agricultural rite incorporated, as were so many others, into the early Christian festivals.

We leave the church through a lych-gate constructed with timbers from the belfry roof damaged when the spire fell. The front of the gate is inscribed with the line 'Rejoice in the Lord alway/And again I say rejoice', together with the music.

Almost opposite the gate are two more buildings notable in the history of the town. First is Hazelbury House, owned by the Packer family, leading clothiers of the late 17c. This three-storeyed Palladian mansion is thought to be the work of John Wood the Younger, whose work and style is dealt with when the route reaches Bath. Further up New Street is the Falcon Hotel. The hotel, which derives its name from the famous falcon on the family crest of the Jerninghams, lords of the manor, was built in 1711, although the bowling-green at the rear is older, having been laid down in the mid-16c. The green was used by the gentlemen of Painswick to while away the idle moment. In times of relative prosperity, Painswick and Stroud had a deep-set rivalry that occasionally spilt over into actual violence. In general the violence was restricted to cock-fights. A *Gloucester Journal* of 1731 records:

Notice is hereby given that on Wednesday 30th of this inst., June, will be fought at the Falcon Inn, in Painswicke, a COCK-MATCH between the Gentlemen of Painswicke and the Gentlemen of Stroud: they are to produce twenty-four cocks, ten of which they are obliged to fight for two Guineas a battle, and ten Guineas the odd battle.

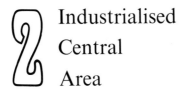

Industrialised Central Area

Painswick to Dursley

The Way continues up Edge Road, opposite the lych-gate, and
through pleasant country to Washbrook Farm. Here the Way is not
at present signposted or waymarked, and it is important not to stray
and bring down the wrath of the owners on all walkers. Go to the R
of the farmhouse and turn L past it. Go round to the R of the barns
and follow a wide track past a new barn on the L. Where the track
goes up R to a gate, continue straight on along an indistinct grass
track to a fence and stile. Follow the path down to the stream and
wooden bridge. Go up the earth and wooden steps to a stile and
over it to the field beyond. Go L towards the old barn and continue
past it to a stile in the fence beyond. From here go L to the road
leading down to Jenkins Farm. This road is followed to the B4072.
The waymarking improves in the route to Scottsquar Hill. The

The quarry on Scottsquar Hill

name is derived from 'sceot', steep, and 'quar', the local short form for quarry. On the hillside, the Way meanders pleasantly through the birch trees, with markers on the trees and an occasional marker post. The path is actually slightly easier to follow going N, and posts have been known to be uprooted, but when intact the arrows show the exact line to the road.   At the road, take the track signposted 'Haresfield Beacon 3 km' which enters another fine broad-leaf wood, beech being interspersed with some horse-chestnut. Watch on the R of the track for a curious hexagonal house set deep in the wood. The track in the wood is followed around the semicircular scarp to emerge near Cliffwell House, next to which stands an old well, whose origin is unknown.

The track now traverses more woodland, passing a stone erected to commemorate the raising of the siege of Gloucester. It is dated 5 September 1643, the day when the Parliamentary army of the Earl

The Cromwell siege stone and Vale of Gloucester

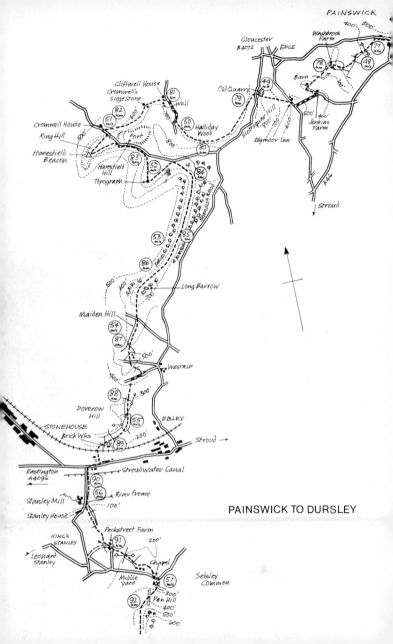

PAINSWICK TO DURSLEY

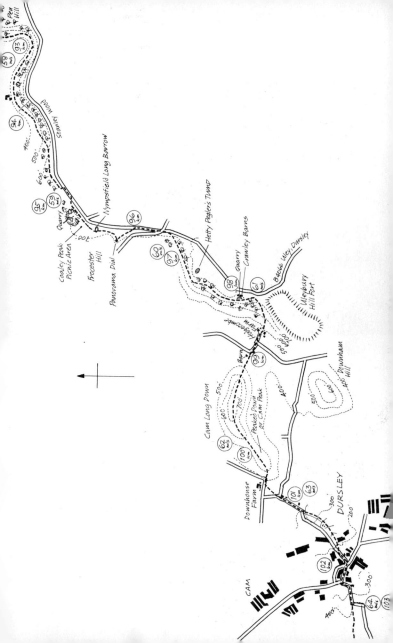

The Cotswold Edge and Severn Vale from Haresfield Beacon

of Essex took Cheltenham before relieving Gloucester, only to find, to their immense pleasure, having spent many hungry, wet days on the march from London, that the King had raised the siege. Why the memorial stone was erected here on the scarp slope of Haresfield Hill is not clear. Locally it is known as Cromwell's Stone and nearby is a house called Cromwell House, suggesting some association as yet not tracked down.

From the end of the woodland track, go L up the road and then R on to a path leading directly to Haresfield Beacon. The Beacon itself is, strictly speaking, only the promontory at the end of Ring Hill. Ring Hill, together with Haresfield Hill to the E, is the site of yet another hill fort in the chain of such structures down to the scarp edge. It is also another that does not have the standard suffix '-bury'. The name is derived from 'Hersa's feld', Hersa's open land, perhaps a reference to the the chieftain who ruled this 16-acre site.

The site is typical of the promontory fort, a spit of land with natural defences on three sides defended across the neck by rampart and ditch. Obviously the site was a good one, and those masters of the arts of war, the Romans, made use of it in their Gloucestershire campaigns. The site has revealed numerous Roman finds, including a hoard of 3,000 coins.

The hill and beacon are most famous for the magnificent view, thought by many to be the best of the Berkeley Vale. In the foreground, the Severn makes its huge meander around Arlingham and broadens considerably, with the Forest of Dean offering a fine backdrop. Also visible are the geological outliers of Robin's Wood Hill and Churchdown. The process of outlier production is seen almost completely in this area, which has the two true outliers mentioned above, the 'only-just' one of Cam Long Down, and the 'soon-will-be' of Haresfield Beacon and Stinchcombe Hill.

After leaving the trig point follow the southern scarp edge back to the E. A little care is needed along the edge of this abrupt drop. The route continues to the right and descends steeply to the R (S). The signpost here is apt to point the wrong way and must be treated with caution. At the bottom of the incline follow the path L (E). A little way along here a stone in the wall to the L is inscribed 'In memory of all foxes killed by the Berkeley Hunt'.

The Way continues out to the panorama dial on a neck of land not named on the maps. The dial is, strictly speaking, a topograph giving an interesting 3D representation of the local area. The topograph has a Cotswold Way arrow that is not entirely successful, the structure being cylindrical. Head NE, to the L of two obvious clumps of trees, to regain the road and Standish Wood. The waymarking is good through the wood that now has conifer plantations amongst the broad-leaves, provided you bear in mind that all the waymarkers are yellow, some of the trees having blue forestry marks.

The wood is ancient, first being recorded in 1297 as belonging to Gloucester Abbey, and leased by it. An interesting sidelight on the creation of surnames is in the note that around 1515 the wood delivered to the Abbey 12 cartloads a year, and that this was delivered by the wood-ward. By 1520 the rents in Standish were

The Cotswold Way in Standish Wood

collected by a family called Woodward, whose head was also
Warden of the Axe. This axe was used to mark those trees that had
been approved of for felling, the penalty for felling others being
severe.

After emerging from Standish Wood, the Way loses character
somewhat as it drops down through the poorly maintained farmland
sometimes associated with suburbs to emerge in the Stroud Valley.
The valley is reached by going over the railway lines next to the
brickworks. Hurry along the A4096 to the road signposted
'Ryeford, Kings Stanley 1, Leonard Stanley 2', and go down it. Pause
by the bridge over the Stroudwater Canal.

The canal symbolises the industrialisation of the Stroud Valley
that started with the wool trade. It was dug from Framilode, to the
NW, where a lock allowed transfer to the Severn, to the centre of
Stroud, thus connecting the town with the Severn and, via the river

Ryeford: The Stroudwater Canal

and the canals in Herefordshire, to the coalfields of Shropshire and Staffordshire. The cheap route for the importation of the new energy source enabled the valley to be more competitive than other local towns and so survive the wool-trade crisis. The canal was not built without difficulties, the local mill-owners objecting, successfully in the early years, on the grounds that water losses, especially in the summer when levels were down, would ruin their businesses. The canal, as completed, was a little over 8 miles long with 12 locks. It was opened in 1779. Soon afterward, a far more ambitious scheme was commenced, the building of the Thames and Severn Canal, with the intention of linking Bristol with London. The starting point was Stroud, and a link was made between the Stroudwater Canal and the Thames nearly 29 miles away. This canal was served by 44 locks, and also by the famous Sapperton Tunnel. The tunnel lies to the east of Stroud and, at 3,817 yards, was the longest in Britain at that time. It was 15 ft wide and 15 ft deep, and kept the navvies – the name for the labourers who dug these navigations – busy for 5 years. Some blasting did take place but, as with the rest of the canals, the main work was with pick and shovel.

Beyond the Stroudwater bridge is another, over the River Frome, beside which is the King's Stanley mill.

The original name was Stanley from 'Stan Leah', the stony clearing, the 'King's' being added later to distinguish this village, the King's, from nearby Leonard Stanley which belonged to the priory of St Leonard. King's Stanley has always been a clothing village, two mills being recorded in Domesday Book which were also the most valuable in the country. The mill passed by the Way, Stanley Mill on the River Frome, was constructed as late as 1811 and was one of the earliest to employ a metal frame to reduce the fire risk. The mill is 5-storeyed, the lowest one of stone, the rest of brick. Initially it was powered by 5 water wheels but in 1827 a steam engine was installed. By the 1830s, the mill employed nearly 1,000 people, including the outdoor weavers, but now the number is down to 250.

A little past the mill is Stanley House, completed in 1593 for the Clutterbuck family, local clothiers. It is an elegant, rectangular stone house, with two storeys and three gables.

The Way turns L on to a footpath just beyond the mill, and then bypasses the village of King's Stanley to reach the village of Middle Yard beyond. King's Stanley itself is typical of the newer, industrialised Cotswold villages. It is useful to backpackers walking the Way because of its shopping facilities. Others may be interested in the church which, though much restored in the 19c, retains some of its Norman features – the base of the tower, and a plain doorway in the northern wall of the nave.

The route to Middle Yard is straightforward except at Peckstreet Farm where, having been directed down and R to a bridge over the stream, there is a great temptation to cross it and continue. But the Way actually goes up again to the opposite corner of the field you came down.

Middle Yard is a pleasant, straggling village on the road to Selsley. The name comes from a house that was built in the 18c in what was then the hamlet of Leighs. Many of the houses are of a similar vintage, late 18c and early 19c, and the plain stone construction, in pairs or in terraces, is typical of the area's weaver cottages.

The Way climbs steeply out of the village up Penn Hill, entering Stanley Wood after a house called, simply, 'The Penn'. On entering the wood, go R and follow a track between waymarked trees. The wood has its difficulties, the waymarking being poor; though the path is obvious, it is set at a high angle, with many protruding tree roots. Care is needed on occasions, especially in wet weather, when it can become treacherous. As with the other woods in the area, however, it is worth the effort, being another fine collection of broad-leaves. At one point the walker leaves the wood to traverse below it for a few hundred yards before re-entering it for the final climb to the top of Frocester Hill. The road at the top of the hill is reached and left again immediately to follow a parallel track through to the Coaley Peak Picnic Site. The site has a small information centre, with wall charts on the local area and its plant and insect life. There is also a diagram of the Nympsfield Long Barrow visible a little way to the SW. The barrow has sadly deteriorated since its first excavation in the mid-19c, and little of the dry-stone walling is now original. Being open to the air, it offers the

Nympsfield Long Barrow on Frocester Hill

opportunity of seeing the general layout of such a burial mound,
Nympsfield being typical of the earlier true-entrance Severn-
Cotswold style. In this case there is only a single pair of side-
chambers from the passageway.

From the long barrow, go S along the fenced scarp edge, taking in
the fine views to Berkeley Vale. The panorama dial at the hill top
shows what to look for. Continue back to the main road and go R
(S) down it. Between here and where the Way rejoins the road at the
Crawley Barns is Hetty Pegler's Tump. This and Belas Knap
represent as fine a pair of long barrows covering the Severn-
Cotswold period as could be found anywhere on the Wolds.
Unfortunately the key to the entrance door that has been fitted to
prevent deterioration is kept at Crawley Barns, which means
backtracking by a little over half a mile from there, or going direct
to the Tump and being unable to look inside. The door is only

about 3 ft high and, though the passage ceiling is a little higher, it is still low. If you have not got a torch, and it is wet, the experience can be unrewarding, if unforgettable.

The name derives from Hester Pegler, the wife of Henry Pegler who owned the field. The couple, who died in 1694 and 1695 respectively, are presumed to have taken an interest in the mound, and perhaps the wife supervised an opening of it. Certainly it has been opened several times, excavations in the 19c revealing fragments of Roman pottery and a silver groat of Edward IV (1461–83). It is believed that the site was dug over in the early 19c by men in search of stone, and subsequent attempts at repair have owed more to enthusiasm than to accuracy. It is thought that the dry-stone walling of the forecourt horns is modern, and that there has been some movement of the upright slabs of the entrance and galleries together, perhaps, with some re-roofing.

The barrow is 140 ft long and 90 ft wide, though its size is partly due to the spread of the covering earth over the original revetment wall. The mound is 10 ft high. Internally there is a 22-ft-long passage about 4 ft wide and 5 ft high with two pairs of side-chambers, both of which on the right-hand (NE and NW) side have been blocked off permanently because of their dangerous state. It is an interesting experience to stand inside the mound, with no light coming in except that through the ancient doorway, and water percolating through the roof and plopping on the slabs. It is easy to believe that there can be a common link joining us with our ancestors, back through 4,500 years.

Whether you reach them via the B4066, or by the wood beneath it, you will come to Crawley Barns. Those coming through the wood should look for the quarry below the barns, which appears at the moment when you are convinced you are on the wrong path. Before descending to Hodgecombe Farm it is worth considering a visit to Uleybury Hill Fort, just S of the barns. This fort, 'Iw Leah Burgh' – the camp at the yew clearing – is a massive site, easily the biggest on the route, enclosing over 30 acres. It is also one of the best protected, with 300-ft scarp drops at all points except the N corner. Further protection is obtained from a single ditch and rampart, though the N corner has extra defences to close off the promontory

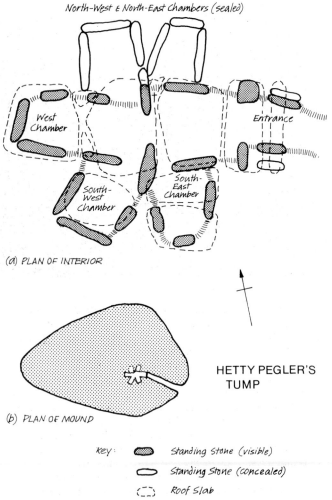

North-West & North-East Chambers (sealed)

West Chamber

Entrance

South-West Chamber

South-East Chamber

(a) PLAN OF INTERIOR

HETTY PEGLER'S TUMP

(b) PLAN OF MOUND

Key:

⬤ Standing Stone (visible)

⬭ Standing Stone (concealed)

⌇ Roof Slab

⫴ Dry-stone Walling

The entrance to Hetty Pegler's Tump

neck. Many experts believe Uleybury to be the finest example of a promontory hill fort in the country, and it is certainly one of the best defensively. No extensive excavation has taken place although there have been several finds, including a gold coin of the Dobunni that is now in Gloucester City Museum.

From Crawley Barns descend to Hodgecombe Farm and then continue up to the summit of Cam Long Down. Though a little less than 700 ft high, the Down commands extensive views because of its position, outlying the scarp edge. Most walkers look forward to its ascent because of the way it draws the eye from Frocester Hill, a height worth scaling. The view looks back to the Edge at Frocester, across to the Forest of Dean and S to Stinchcombe Hill.

The Down itself has a plateau summit that is carved with curious ridges and troughs. These, together with flints discovered here, suggest a settlement in the distant past, though not a defended hill

The view ahead to Cam Long Down from Hodgecombe Farm

fort in the accepted sense. The name 'Cam' is from crooked, which is descriptive of the Down. Local legend has it that it was the work of the Devil who, taking a dislike to Gloucestershire because of the high ratio of churches to acres, decided that he would flood the county by damming the Severn. To do this he needed stones, and these he obtained from a quarry near Dursley. Having filled his wheelbarrow, he sat down to rest. As he rested, a cobbler came along the road carrying, round his neck, a string of worn-out shoes awaiting repair. The Devil asked the cobbler how far it was to the Severn. The cobbler, smelling a rat, pointed to the string of shoes and said that he had worn them all out on his journey from there. The Devil thereupon tipped all the stones out of his barrow, and Cam Long Down was formed.

The Way traverses the Down and descends to Cam Peak, with its curious ironwork on the summit. To this structure a cross is tied each Easter when the townspeople of Dursley and Cam come here to celebrate the Passion. Descend from the Peak to reach the road at Downhouse Farm. Here the Way cuts the corner by crossing a field but, if the weather is bad, the field can be very muddy and it is easier to follow the road around. Follow the road until a path leads off L, allowing the last few hundred yards into Dursley to be crossed via farmland. On this section, at Home Farm, the Way passes a very fine example of a Cotswold stone barn with hay-loft.

Description of route continues on p. 162.

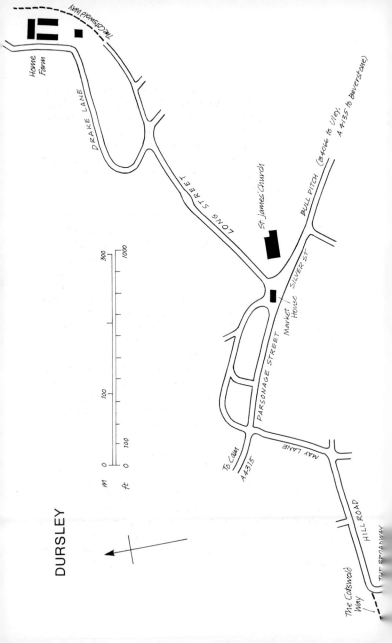

Dursley, along with Wotton, has made a successful transition from old Cotswold wool town to modern town. The change has not been entirely due to its proximity to Bristol with the consequent increase in commuter population, but also to the setting up of local industries so that the town is not just a dormitory for Bristol workers but a thriving community. The price that has been paid is a modernisation that has affected much of the old wool town, a change that must be viewed realistically.

The town is beautifully situated between two spurs of the Cotswolds, to the N Downham Hill, Cam Peak and Cam Long Down, and to the S the most westerly of the spurs, Stinchcombe Hill. The vale so formed is fed by the Ewelme Brook that becomes the River Cam beyond the town boundary. It is not surprising, in view of the sheltered situation and the water supply, that the area should have been settled early. The name Dursley is the modern form of 'Dersilege', which is believed to be derived from 'Dearsige's Leah', Dearsige's clearing, named after an Anglo-Saxon leader. It is known, however, that this habitation was late in the area's history since it contains Roman as well as Neolithic remains.

By the time of Domesday, the manor of Dursley was owned by Roger de Berkeley, possessor of one of the names that is so famous in the Severn Vale W of Dursley. Roger was a cousin of Edward the Confessor and so had royal English blood as well as being a Norman Lord of Dursley – a formidable combination. He had a castle built at Dursley of which nothing remains but the name 'Castle Fields' in the NW part of the town. The family prospered under the Normans and, in the spirit of the times, endowed several religious houses, Roger founding the St Leonards Priory at Leonard Stanley, and his nephew and successor, William, a monastery at Kingswood near Wotton-under-Edge. The prosperity received a setback, however, when Henry I died and the family backed Stephen in the civil war that followed. William was captured by the armies of Matilda and the Earl of Gloucester and died in prison. His son, another Roger, escaped but, when Henry II was acknowledged King, he, being Matilda's son, stripped the Berkeleys of their estates and

passed them to Robert Fitzharding. The same qualities that had
allowed the family to become assimilated into the Norman system
showed themselves again when Roger Berkeley's daughter Alice
married Robert Fitzharding's son Maurice. This manipulated
marriage succeeded in regaining some family estates, Henry II
making it a condition of the marriage that Roger Berkeley regained
his Dursley castle and lands, and besides this the Fitzhardings,
having been installed in Berkeley Castle, decided to take the name
Berkeley for themselves. The family still lives in Berkeley Castle,
representing an unbroken line of 900 years back to the Norman
Conquest.

Those interested in the history of the family and its position
in local history may visit the castle which is open, normally, between
late March and September daily except on Mondays, and on
Sundays only in October.

By the late 15c Dursley was sharing the new-found Cotswold wool
and cloth prosperity. One of the reasons for the share of the market
that Dursley had seems to be the residence in the town of a family
named Webb. Before the building up of the English – mainly
Cotswold – wool trade, English wool was exported to Holland and
there made into superb cloth, far better than any that was at the
time made in England. It was not long before the English royal
house realised that such a procedure made bad economic sense.
Consequently the court sent out an agent who managed to convince
some of the Dutch under-masters that they would be better off as
masters in England. The Dutch craftsmen were promised fat beef
and mutton, profits, good beds and better bed-fellows. The latter
offer implied that the rich English, with an eye to the main chance,
would encourage their daughters to marry the Dutch. It was also
stated that the daughters concerned were of such beauty 'that the
most envious foreigners could not but commend them'.

Whichever of the offers – meat, money or daughters – was the
most persuasive, the effect was a migration of Dutch craftsmen to
England. In order to prevent any malcontent from persuading the
others to go back home, they were spread widely throughout
England, and some were settled in the Cotswolds. Some of the
craftsmen were given English surnames for better absorption into

the social structure and one of the prime cloth-makers, who had settled in Gloucestershire, was given the name Webb. Almost certainly it was this Webb who assisted Dursley in obtaining a large share of the cloth market. The name Webb was given because of his craft, a 'webb' being a roll of cloth. Within a short time, the Webbs had become the leading family in the town, and the clothing interest they began lasted until the early 20c when there were still clothiers of the name in nearby Nailsworth.

The trade was not always carried on in the most ethical manner. By the 15c it had become proverbial that a Dursley man was a cheat, and the expression 'You are a man of Dursley' was used as a term of abuse. The first trick the townsmen thought up was to sell cloth folded so that it concealed a portion that was badly coloured or woven, or to conceal a short width. When this was made illegal by act of Parliament, they moved on to stretching the cloth to increase the yardage, a system that required the application of 'flock' powder to restore the thickness. The procedure became so notorious that eventually Bishop Latimer himself was moved to condemn stretching and filling with 'devil's dust' in a sermon.

In the long term, the fate of Dursley was the same as that of all the wool towns, the depression in trade causing unemployment and poverty. The response to the problem in the town was a little different from that in others: the setting up of a house of industry – the workhouse. At this remove from the times of the mid-18c and early 19c, it is difficult to be objective about such institutions, but it does seem that on the whole the system worked, offering a little hope for the otherwise hopeless. As always, the tragedy was not the workhouse, but the system that made its establishment necessary. The Dursley institution was run on the standard rules of cleanliness, godliness and stern discipline, but it did have a dormitory set aside for the old and infirm, a section of the community whose fate then was bleak elsewhere. In this dormitory in 1806 an old man in his eighties hanged himself, a sad occurrence made sadder by the reason for it. He was one of the 6 marines who in 1757 had formed the firing-squad at the execution of Admiral Byng. 49 years later the long-held conviction that it had been his musket that had fired the fatal shot became too much for him to bear.

The setting up of a workhouse indicates that Dursley had no intention of abdicating its role as prosperous country town, even if it had fallen on hard times. An example of this is recorded in the local liking for alliterative names, and with Proud Painswick and Strutting Stroud we have Drunken Dursley. Whereas some of the other Cotswold wool towns declined, both in wealth and population, Dursley shifted the emphasis of its industry to cope with the altered situation.

The most important of the newer industries was that set up as R. A. Lister and Co. in the mid-19c, which exists still as a world-famous manufacturer of diesel engines. Some of the company's early success was due to a Dane called Mikael Pedersen who appeared in Dursley around 1890 and disappeared again around the time of the Great War. Pedersen was an inventor of genius who produced various agricultural designs, but concentrated on the creation of the perfect bicycle. His bicycles were made by Listers in the early years, and were remarkable for their curious designs and their price, some costing more than the equivalent of £200 in modern terms. He was one of the first to offer gearing, a 3-speed hub gear being produced in 1902 with a friction clutch. This far-sighted attempt failed and was replaced by a toothed drive, but the name Dursley-Pedersen was renowned for quality. In 1900 one of the cycles was used to break the record for the London-to-York ride, and to set up world records for 100 miles and for 12 hours. On each occasion the rider was Harry Green. At the start of the war Pedersen worked on military equipment, and then disappeared. The photographs that exist show him to be a perfect example of the talented eccentric, with a huge black beard set below kindly features.

The prize for remaining a 'living' town was the destruction of most of the old buildings and their replacement with those more suited to the new working generation. Most of the buildings in the town are therefore from the early 19c onwards. Two notable exceptions are on the route: the Market House and, opposite it, the church. These buildings will be described later.

In addition to its success as a prosperous country town, Dursley has also produced men who have touched English history, if only lightly. Edward Fox who, as Bishop of Hereford, was a contributor to the Reformation, and was also the man who introduced Cranmer to Henry VIII, was born here. Dursley also gave the world William King, who, by his setting up of Sunday school in the town, is credited with starting the Sunday School movement.

Neither has Dursley neglected a role in the arts. There is strong evidence that Shakespeare lived in the town in 1585 when hiding from Sir Thomas Lucy, who wished to have words with him regarding certain poached deer. There were certainly Shakespeares in the area at the time, one of them having been buried at Bisley in 1570, and they were present until recent times. Conclusive evidence of William Shakespeare's residence is lacking, but is implied in a line in *Henry IV, Part Two*, Act V, Scene i, which refers to Woncot – the vernacular rendering even now of Woodmancote – and to men known to have lived in the area: Visor, the Dursley bailiff, and Clement Perkes who lived, as the line says, on the hill (Stinchcombe

Dursley: Long Street from the Market House

Hill). Another line, in *Richard II*, refers to the view of Berkeley Castle 'by yon tuft of trees', implying that the poet had seen the castle from the top of Stinchcombe Hill. Indeed, there is a walk in Hermitage Wood, on that part of the hill immediately SW of the wood, still known as Shakespeare's Walk.

The Market House is an oddly-shaped building set like a roundabout in the middle of the junction of four roads, its age more obvious because it is surrounded by modern shop fronts. It was erected in 1738 by the Estcourt family, who were by then lords of the manor. The Berkeleys had been succeeded in that position first by the Wykes and then by the Estcourts, the Berkeley line continuing at Berkeley Castle. The arms of the Estcourts can be seen on the S front, the E front having a recessed statue of Queen Anne. Dursley had been granted a market by Henry VIII, but this building appears to have been the first permanent covered area. The house has an upper room, reached by the stairs in one corner, which was used originally as the County court. In addition, a fire-bell inscribed 'Come away without delay' was installed in 1747 to rouse the firemen, then voluntary, to action. The new station is still only 100 yards or so to the N of the house. The building was for a long time maintained in a reasonable state of repair and was used as a communal kitchen in the 1939–45 war, but in the early fifties it fell into a sad state, possibly due to the lack of acceptable plumbing.

As is often the case, the decay of the building was only arrested when it was suggested that it should be demolished to make way for a road. It was promptly renovated and modernised and is now a real part of the community again.

Opposite the Market House is the church, a jigsaw puzzle of a building, with contributions from numerous architectural styles spread over many centuries. There is some doubt as to when the first church was erected in Dursley, although it does not appear to have been earlier than the mid-12c. The first reference is in 1221, when it is recorded that sanctuary was sought there by a murderer. The man had killed a woman and escaped from his imprisonment in Berkeley Castle. His fleeing to Dursley rather than to the nearby Berkeley church implies that Dursley was, by then, a sanctuary church of repute. The process of seeking sanctuary was not, as is sometimes assumed, a complete escape from punishment. The seeker, after he had confessed his crime in sanctuary, was banished for ever from the area. He then went without shoes and hat, carrying a cross, to the nearest port, where he walked into the water up to his knees as a gesture of his intention to accept banishment overseas.

Little is left of the original church: six corbels in 'Tanner's Chapel' and the upper slab of a priest's grave with an indistinct cross at the foot of the stairs leading to the parvis, or priest's room. This can be seen just inside the small doorway near the font.

In the early 14c, the church was almost completely rebuilt. Of this period more remains, including the octagonal column arcades and the splendid sedilia or sanctuary seats near the altar. The original tower had been left intact during this rebuilding but, in 1480, a new tower, complete with clock, peal of bells and spire was constructed.

Now the church has a tower, but no longer a spire. By the time Defoe, in his 17c tour of Britain, referred to it as being 'handsome', the spire seems to have already been giving cause for concern. After several attempts to shore it up from the inside, it was decided to have it extensively repaired in early 1698. To that end 52 hundredweight of lead was purchased (for £37. 17s.) and this, together with 9 'loads' of tiles, was used to renovate it. The work was completed and on the 7 January a celebration peal of the bells was rung. The weight of the lead and the vibrations caused by the bell-ringing were too much for the spire, which, 'by casualty and great Mischance fell downe'. Fortunately it fell outwards rather than through the nave but, even so, the end wall of the church was pulled down and several people were killed. The damage was reckoned at £1,995. 0s. 9d., a colossal sum by the standards of the day. It was too much for the town to bear, and a petition was made to the King for the money to rebuild. Eventually, after many years, the petition was granted by Queen Anne, which also explains why her statue is on the nearby Market House. The grant was insufficient for total rebuilding and, when the work was completed in 1709, the church had a tower, but no steeple.

Even the reconstruction of the tower was not the last major rebuilding work carried out; in 1867 the old chancel was demolished and a new one, larger and higher, was erected. After that there was major work on the windows but there were no further structural changes.

The interior of the church is notable for the number, and lack of great interest, of its wall plaques. The chapel known as Tanner's Chapel on the S side of the church does contain a memorial of note, an effigy of Thomas Tanner who endowed the chantry in the mid-15c. The effigy is headless, and has been for some time, and is curious for its wasted appearance. If it is a true likeness then Tanner must have been in poor shape when it was modelled.

Dursley to Wotton-under-Edge

The Way leaves Dursley via May Lane and Hill Road, from which it breaks away R into the wooded climb up Stinchcombe Hill. This wood has been the centre of attention lately over the gassing of badgers, undertaken, so it is said, to prevent the spread of bovine tuberculosis. The wood at the time of this operation was dotted with warning notices and, though it is at present clear, it is advisable to keep to the obvious, though rough, path.

At the top is yet another golf course. Those who are disinclined can miss out the 2 miles to Drakestone Point and back, but the superb views make the effort worthwhile. The Way is well signposted across the golf course, turning off the main path at a car park and passing just in front of one tee. Eventually a shelter erected to the memory of Sir Stanley William Tubbs, who gave the land to the public, is reached. From here, and even more so from the nearby Drakestone Point, the highest point of the hill, the views are superb. The hill is only a little over 700 ft high, but it compensates by having open views for about 240 degrees of its viewing circle. This is due to the hill's curious T-shape, of which the 'horizontal' is over a mile long, and the 'vertical' in places only a few yards across. It is therefore possible to look almost due SE into Waterley Bottom, as well as N along the scarp edge. The view down into Stinchcombe village immediately below shows its fine setting in 'Stint Cumb', or 'Sandpiper Valley'. On clear days it is possible to see Exmoor and the Brecon Beacons, as well as the familiar Malverns, and the route S is visible as far as the Somerset monument at Hawkesbury Upton, 12 walking miles away.

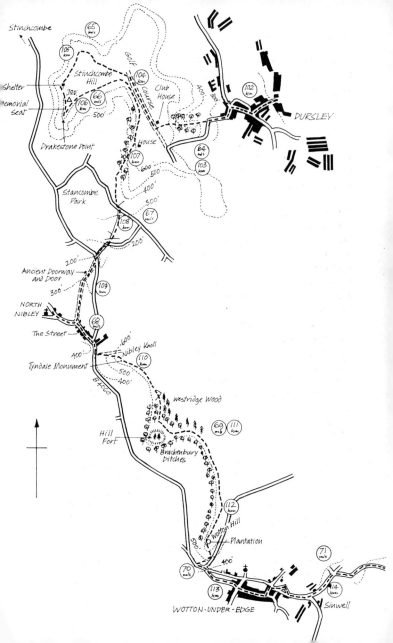

Stinchcombe

65 km's

105 km

Golf Course

Stinchcombe Hill

104 km

Club House

102 km

DURSLEY

shelter

Memorial Seat

700'

106 km

66 m'ls

500'

Drakestone Point

House

64 m'ls

107 km

600'

103 km

500'

400'

Stancombe Park

500'

108 km

67 m'ls

200'

200'

Ancient Doorway and Door

300'

109 km

NORTH NIBLEY

68 m'ls

The Street

600'

Nibley Knoll

110 km

Tyndale Monument

400'

500'

400'

Westridge Wood

60 m'ls

111 km

Hill Fort

Brackenbury Ditches

112 km

Wotton Hill

Plantation

500'

71 m'ls

70 m'ls

400'

113 km

114 km

Sinwell

WOTTON-UNDER-EDGE

The Way now returns towards the club house. The waymarking here is not excellent and care must be taken not to go too far S to finish on a small spur of land offering good views down into Hollow Combe but poor prospects of further progress. A path to the R (S) is taken, just before a house, down through the wood to a stream that can be passed by descending the steps or, for the more intrepid, by balancing across the gas pipe. Continue across fields to the road.

Opposite is a lane leading up to North Nibley, notable in late spring for its powerful smell of wild garlic. Note the old doorway to the R (W) dated 1607. There is no trace behind it of what it once opened on to.

North Nibley is another '-ley' village, the suffix denoting a clearing in the wood. In this southern part of the route around Wotton, the names of many villages end in this way, implying heavy afforestation. The prefix is from 'Hnybba', a peak, the village being set high on the scarp with a prominent knoll. The 'North' is to distinguish it from Nibley near Westerleigh. The route goes L (SE) from the top of the lane, but there is much of interest to the R. First is the church of St Martin, a fine building in the Early English and Perpendicular styles. The interior is striking for the beautiful vaulted ceiling supported by corbels of Kings and Queens. The heads are good, but the beards of the Kings give them a curious, seal-like look. The S wall has a painted relief statue of Grace Smith, who died in 1609, which stands below an arch with painted coats of arms. The chancel is elegantly, if somewhat monotonously, painted with a simple floral motif and a more elaborate leaf-design border. The churchyard contains the tombs of several members of the Tyndale family believed to be descended from that of William Tyndale whose monument dominates the local landscape.

Below the church is Nibley Green, where the last pitched battle on English soil between private armies was fought in 1470. Remarkably, this event was the sad outcome of the enduring love of Thomas, Lord Berkeley for his wife. Their lives and tombs will be discussed at Wotton. Following the death of his wife, Thomas did not remarry and died heirless, his daughter Elizabeth having married Richard Beauchamp, Earl of Warwick. Consequently his title passed to his nephew, and there was, almost immediately, trouble over the rightful ownership of the great Berkeley estates. Various acts of villainy ensued, Lord Berkeley forcing an envoy to eat his parchment letter, including the waxed seal, for which he spent a few days in the Tower, and the opposition breaking into Berkeley Castle to hold the Berkeleys hostage for a while. Various lawsuits followed, to the satisfaction of neither side. Finally Thomas Talbot, Lord Lisle, a grandson of the Countess of Warwick and of John Talbot, lord of the manor of Painswick (whose death in France, as we have noted, was mentioned by Shakespeare), decided to settle the feud. He was only 20 at the time, and hot-headed enough to challenge the new Lord Berkeley, William, direct.

> I require thee of knighthood and of manhood to appoint a day to meet me halfway [between Lisle's house at Wotton and Berkeley Castle], there to try between God and our two hands, all our quarrel and title of right, for to eschew the shedding of Christian men's blood, or else at the same day bring the utmost of thy power, and I shall meet thee.

He goes on to talk of 'all your carts of gunnes, bowes, with other ordnance . . . to bete it down upon my head'. The same day Berkeley, much annoyed by the challenge, replied:

> Thomas Talbot, otherwise called Viscount Lisle, not long continued in that name, but a new found thing, brought out of strange countrys . . . I will thou understand not bring the tenth part that I can make, and I will appoint a short day to ease thy malicious heart and thy false counsell that is with thee; fail not tomorrow to be at Niblyes Green at eight or nine of the clock, and I will not fail, with God's might and grace to meet thee at the same place.

And so, on 20 March 1470, each man arrived with about 1,000 retainers. The action was swift, a single charge of Lisle's men into what may have been an ambush. About 150 men were killed, including the young Lord Lisle, whose house was sacked by the Berkeley men after they had finished pursuing the remnants of his fleeing army over the country. In typical style, the killer of Lisle was duly named, one Black Will, a forester from Lydney. Lisle, having been shot in the face, was finished off with a dagger stroke. Typically, the battle solved nothing, dispute and litigation continuing for several hundred years.

The Way ascends Nibley Knoll by a footpath off the main Wotton road; at the bottom of the hill is a board giving the whereabouts of the key to the Tyndale monument on the Knoll, for those who wish to climb it for the views it affords. The true Way leaves this path after 100 yards or so to climb up a steep slope, this being the right of way; the wide track that leads to the knoll top, from which it is possible to return by the footpath to the tower, is not. The tower was erected in 1866 as a memorial to William Tyndale, the translator of the Bible, whose life will be dealt with in the section on Little Sodbury. The plaque states that he was born near this spot,

The Tyndale Monument on Nibley Knoll

although there are good arguments for believing he was born at either Slimbridge or Cam.

From the tower, follow the scarp edge around to Westridge Wood. In the wood the waymarking is excellent, which is as well as there is a complex array of paths. In spring the wood is full of bluebells and fine trees. About halfway through it, the Way traverses the defended promontory neck of the hill fort known as Brackenbury Ditches. The fort is overgrown with trees that have prevented excavation, but have not obscured the size and defences of the site. The fort covers about 6 acres, in the form of a triangle, with the scarp slope as defence on two sides, accentuated by ramparts, and the neck heavily defended. The neck defence is huge, consisting of a double ditch and rampart with a wide, interlying berm. Because the site is so quiet, being well shielded by the woodland, the walker penetrating deeply into it is conscious of its silence and solitude. For that reason its great size is apparent and the site possesses more character than the technically superior ones at Uleybury and Old Sodbury.

Continue through the wood and cross a field to emerge on Wotton Hill. Here there is a walled plantation of trees planted in 1815 to celebrate Waterloo, felled and burnt as a bonfire to celebrate the end of the Crimean War, and replanted in 1887 to celebrate the jubilee of Queen Victoria. Much earlier, in the reign of Edward I, the hill was used to play stool-ball, that game that may have been the ancestor of golf or cricket, or of both, played with a hard leather ball stuffed with feathers and a stick $3\frac{1}{2}$ ft long.

Descend steeply, S from the plantation to pick up a path that leads down to the road. Go L (E) and enter Wotton.

Description of route continues on p. 181.

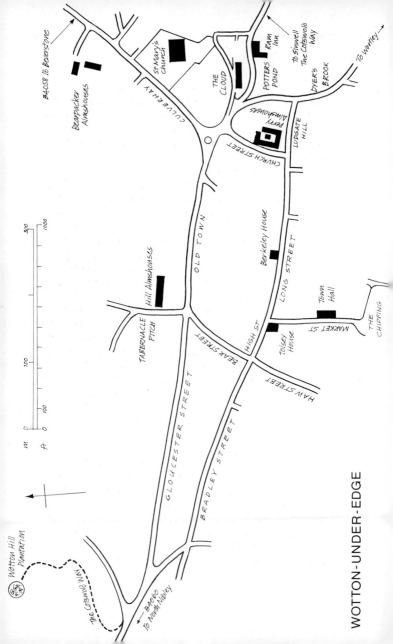

WOTTON-UNDER-EDGE

Wotton was 'Wudu tun', the farm in the wood, in Saxon times, the suffix 'under Edge' being added around the 14c to accentuate its position below the Cotswold Edge. The area around Wotton must have been very thickly wooded, since many of the local villages – Alderley, Hillesley, Wortley, Nibley – bear the suffix 'ley', from 'leah', a clearing.

The first record of the town dates, as would be expected, from Saxon times, a royal charter of 940 mentioning the leasing of land – 4 hides, equalling 480 acres – to Thegn, or Thane, Edric from the King of Wessex, Edmund. Following the Norman Conquest, the town, then no more than a village, became part of the Berkeley estate. During the era of problems over the ownership of the estate, as mentioned in the section on Dursley, Wotton did surprisingly well. At one time during the in-fighting between the Berkeleys, Thomas Berkeley, being excluded from his castle, promptly built a manor house at Wotton and raised its status by including Nibley and Wortley in the manor. This original village was in the part now known as Old Town, and was destroyed by fire in the reign of King John. It is thought that the fire was deliberately set as a reprisal for the part played by Lord Berkeley, the second Robert, in the events leading up to Magna Carta. Robert was certainly one of the leaders of the barons' movement, although the idea that their last meeting prior to the presentation of their demands was at Berkeley, though widely promoted, is incorrect. The meeting was in fact at Brackley.

Following the fire, the town was rebuilt and grew to become one of the most important of the Cotswold wool towns. There were mills along the stream that runs through Potters Pond which is, aptly, named Dyers Brook. By the early 1600s the town was well established in the trade, assisted, as Dursley had been, by the influx of Flemish clothiers. A census taken in 1608 showed that, of the town's work-force, half were employed in the clothing trade. The trades of the others give an interesting view of Wotton's life. There were 21 shoemakers, 2 bakers, 5 butchers, 5 glovers, a barber, an apothecary, 4 innkeepers, 7 carpenters, a chandler, 6 smiths, 4 masons, a glazier, a tiler, a hooper, 6 millers, 3 tanners and 5 carriers.

Such was the prosperity of the town in the early 17c. By the early 19c, however, it had declined, as had all the others, and had seen its share of the problems caused by the shrinkage of the profits in the wool trade. There were serious riots in 1825 which caused the final demise of an already dying local trade. Wotton, like Dursley, successfully underwent the change from a town with a wool-trade past to a town with a future, and is now a thriving community with local industry as well as Bristol commuters. In making the transition, the town also managed to keep more of the architectural treasures than elsewhere, so that it has a recognisable older section, though some of this has been modified to meet modern requirements.

The Cotswold Way enters Wotton via Bradley Street. In the early 19c, there was a Wesleyan school in this street which, in 1836, acquired a famous teacher. Isaac Pitman was born in 1813, the second of 11 children of a clerk in a Trowbridge clothing factory. After becoming a teacher, his first job was on Humberside, but he accepted the Wotton job to return to the West of England. The story runs that, on the journey south, he fell into religious discussions with a man from Clifton who altered his convictions. Consequent on this change, he was sacked from the teaching post after a short time, the local Wesleyan minister telling the congregation that 'if he held such religious sentiments he should expect to be hunted out of the town like a mad dog'. Pitman left the chapel and joined the Church of England. He also set up his own school in Wotton in January 1837, which he ran until 1839. During this period he invented his shorthand system, which he taught to his pupils. A plaque on his old house in Orchard Street reads 'In this house Sir Isaac Pitman, b 1813, d 1897, invented his System of Shorthand known as Phonography in the year 1837'.

Crossing into High Street and Long Street, a number of interesting houses come into view. To the R, the National Westminster Bank is housed in a fine early 18c house with 3 storeys and a top parapet. The bank first leased the house in 1851. To the L is an interesting doorway with a wooden lintel cut in the style of a Tudor arch with cusps. Further down on the L is the White Lion Inn, first mentioned in 1610, although most of the old building is concealed behind the modern red brick.

On the R, on the corner of Market Street, is Tolsey House. The house was built originally in the late 16c, although there has been considerable rebuilding and renovation, and it has had a variety of uses. It started out as the Court House, the site of the Pie Powder court. This Court, Curia Pedis Pulverizati, the court of Piepoudre – dusty feet – was set up to deal with cases connected with those attending markets and fairs, literally those with dusty feet, the travelling traders. The house has also probably served as a prison, there being evidence of a prison cell in the cellar which is itself cut into the bedrock. On the roof is an elegant bell-turret topped with a superb weathervane in the shape of a dragon, complete with spiky tail and forked tongue. The vane, which is of copper, was added in 1707, but may have been renewed in 1859. The clock was added to celebrate the Jubilee of Queen Victoria.

The turning to the R here, Market Street, leads to the old market which is still called Chipping, as in Chipping Campden. The street itself is very ancient. The W side still retains 16c timbered houses, while the E side contains the Town Hall. This is an 18c building which was once a covered market. The market cover was supported by the still visible Doric columns. The building was converted for use as a Town Hall in the late 19c. The E side has undergone recent major reconstruction, a scheme that was felt to have succeeded so well in retaining the original character that it gained an architectural award in 1975.

Returning to Long Street the route continues eastwards along it, passing many shops whose upper halves are of architectural interest. Note the large kettle swinging high above the pavement as a reminder of the times when all shopkeepers had such signs of their trades. Long Street also contains what is perhaps the most famous of Wotton's houses, Berkeley House. This is a largely unspoilt 17c Jacobean house. The name is something of misnomer, since there is no known connection with the Berkeley family. It seems to have arisen as late as 1922 when the house was described, by a somewhat over-enthusiastic agent at a time of selling, as 'one time property of the Berkeley family'. The exterior of the house, being in its original stone condition, is very fine, but it was the interior that attracted fame. In 1924 a room of the house was bought by the Victoria and

Wotton-under-Edge: Market Street

Albert Museum, and erected there complete. The room was panelled
with green-painted pine, above which was wallpaper painted with
birds, trees and flowers in Chinese style. It also contained a fine
chimneypiece and surround of decorated plaster, the whole having
been put together between 1740 and 1760. There are two similar
rooms in the county, one at Painswick House and the other at
Hardwick Court. Each of these is later, however, and each has been
affected by the sun. An earlier, oak-panelled room in Berkeley House
was sold to the USA. The house has many other points of interest,
including a small stone tablet depicting 3 'genii loci', a 'genius loci'
being a guardian spirit for the building. Next door to the house is
another with a stone dated 1748, with the initials 'ESW'. These stand
for Elizabeth and Susanna Wallington, daughters of a long-standing
Wotton family.

On reaching the bottom of Long Street, turn L, rather than going
down the familiarly named Ludgate Hill, into Church Street. Here
on the R is the 17c Falcon Hotel beside which are the Perry
Almshouses, perhaps Wotton's finest memorial to its wool-trade
past. Hugh Perry was born in Wotton and became an extremely
rich merchant and mercer in London where he was sheriff in 1632.
On his death in 1634 he was given a monument in St
Bartholomew's, which was destroyed in the Great Fire. Perry's
daughter Mary married Henry Noel, the second son of Viscount
Campden, whose family has already been noted in Chipping
Campden. The story of her marriage suggests that even in those
days wealth did not necessarily bring success. Shortly after the
marriage, the couple's house was besieged in the Civil War by
Parliamentary soldiers. Mary assisted in the defence of the house,
melting lead for bullets, but eventually the family surrendered and
the house was plundered. The couple were imprisoned and Mary,
who was pregnant, contracted smallpox which caused a late
miscarriage. She also infected Henry, who died soon after. This all
happened in less than one year of marriage, and Mary's later life
was not much of an improvement, her second husband dying and
leaving her with a young family.

Hugh Perry made several endowments to the town, one being a
water conduit providing the town centre with its first water supply.

He left £300 in his will for the erection of an almshouse with gardens and accommodation for 6 poor men and 6 poor women. A further £250 was bequeathed to provide £12 a year for distribution to these 12, and £1 for an annual dinner for the trustees when picking new beneficiaries. The houses, constructed in 1638 of small undressed stones, are an excellent example of Cotswold architecture of the period. Visitors are welcome to pass through the frontage to the quiet quadrangle inside. There is a tiny chapel, also provided from the £300. The S wing of the houses was added in 1712 with a bequest in the will of Thomas Dawes, a buyer in the wool trade.

The town is remarkable for its number of almshouses. Those at the top of Culverhay, opposite Church Street, were founded in 1837 by Miss Ann Bearpacker, the heiress of one of the local moneyed families. She left the site and £3,000 for 10 poor and infirm members of the Church of England, each of whom was to receive 3 shillings a week after attending Tuesday morning service. In the NW part of the town, in Tabernacle Pitch, are the Hill Almshouses, founded in the 19c as a memorial to the Rev. Rowland Hill who founded the Tabernacle Chapel opposite the houses.

Church Street is believed to have been the site of the grammar school founded by Katharine, Lady Berkely in 1384, making it one of the oldest in the country. Although the site of the school has changed several times, the name of Katharine Lady Berkeley is still given to the modern school on the Kingswood road, maintaining a 600-year history of education. One of its more famous pupils was Dr Edward Jenner, the pioneer of vaccination.

At the end of Church Street, go across the main road to The Cloud, probably named, like Cleeve Cloud, from 'clud', a rock or bluff. Down to the R from here is the Ram Inn, believed to be Wotton's oldest house. It is thought that the builders of the church were housed here, and the church was completed in 1283. The house was originally timber-framed, but was later encased in stone. It was in a very poor condition when bought by the present owner, who is restoring it gradually. Though no longer an inn, it is now a guest house. The Ram stands in an area known as Potters Pond, incorrectly named on the Ordnance Survey 1:25000 sheet ST79 as Potters Pound. The error seems to have occurred because the old town pound is nearby, the site being known as Pound's Ground.

At the end of The Cloud is the church of St Mary the Virgin, Wotton's parish church. It is thought that the site was an ancient one and, although there is no mention of the church in Domesday Book, it is likely that there was in fact a Norman church, since there exist records of 12c Norman vicars. The earliest known date, however, is for an induction in 1283 and some sections of the church date from then, although much has been rebuilt and extended, notably in the 15c. The tower, which is believed by many to be the finest in Gloucestershire, is a composite, a 15c section surmounting a 14c lower section, including the W door. This door is not the entrance, the church being entered by the S door. Here there is a 13c porch which was rebuilt in the 17c, when a priest's chamber was constructed above it. This chamber formerly housed a considerable library of theological books, but these have been rehoused in Christ Church, Oxford because of their age and value.

The main body of the church is remarkably large, owing, in part, to the aisles being as wide as the nave. It is also remarkable for the number and quality of the carvings. Note particularly the tiny sculpted heads above the columns supporting the aisle archways. These are probably 19c, as is the most unusual, the hood stop on the archway to the vestry from the N aisle. This depicts a silent woman, silent because of very effective gagging. The N aisle has an excrescence, the term being applied to a passage leading to an additional chapel. In this case it is believed that there was a chapel dedicated to St Katherine in the churchyard, and the passage that led to it was converted to the present chapel when the original chapel was lost. Digging in the churchyard in the mid-19c revealed many broken tiles believed to have been from the chapel, some depicting St Katherine's wheel and others the Berkeley arms. The current chapel bears the name 'Katharine', a spelling identical with that of Katharine, Lady Berkeley. It is likely, though, that, since St Katherine was the patron saint of weavers, the dedication was to her, the spelling being an acceptable rendering of the saint's name. The fireplace dates from around 1800, when the chapel was used as the vestry. The oak roof was added as late as 1928 when the chapel had fallen into a poor state of repair.

The N aisle also houses, at the E end, a marble tomb chest containing the superb life-size brasses of Thomas, Lord Berkeley and his wife Margaret. It is believed that the brasses date from around 1392 when Margaret died, making the brass one of the earliest in the county. It is arguably also the finest, and almost certainly the most famous. Thomas, the 10th Lord Berkeley and the fourth Thomas, was born at the family castle in 1352. He accompanied Richard II in his war against the Scots, but later, in 1399, was a key figure in deposing him in favour of Henry IV. Following this he was made Warden of the Welsh Marches and Admiral of the Fleet, and in this latter capacity he was responsible for the defeat of Owen Glendower's French allies off Milford Haven. He fought in several campaigns in France, and was with Henry V at the battle of Agincourt in 1415, by which time he was 63. He died in 1417.

Despite the apparently arranged nature of the marriage (Margaret was 7, Thomas 14 at the time), the Berkeleys were obviously very happy. Margaret died in 1392 at the age of about 30 and Thomas appears to have been grief-stricken. It is certainly true that he never remarried, presumably in deference to her memory, since he had no male heir, their only child being a daughter, Elizabeth, who married Richard, Earl of Warwick. The deep love he had for his wife is mirrored in Thomas's inscription on the tomb:

In youth our parents joyn'd our hands, our selves, our hearts,
This tombe our bodyes hath, th'heavens our better parts.

It is a pity that such a loving relationship should eventually lead to tragedy, the battle at Nibley Green being a direct result of Thomas's lack of a male heir.

The brass is particularly noteworthy for Lord Berkeley's collar with its mermaids, and also for the remarkable resemblance the dog at Lady Margaret's feet bears to the one on the brass of Lady Isobel Russel at Dyrham church, which will be seen later on the route. It is believed that both brasses were the work of one man, a belief strengthened by the dating of the Russel memorial to 1401. For those wishing to make a rubbing, replicas of the brass are available,

Wotton-under-Edge: The 15c tower of St Mary's Church

Wotton-under-Edge: The memorial brass to Thomas, Lord Berkeley, St Mary's Church

Wotton-under-Edge: The memorial brass to Margaret, Lady Berkeley, St Mary's Church

one in the church itself and another in the St Nicholas Church Museum in Bristol.

An older memorial lies in the floor beneath the tower. This, from which the brass has unfortunately been stolen, dates from 1329 and is to Richard de Wotton, a vicar of the church. The remaining matrix portrays a kneeling priest beneath a cross with a picture of the Virgin. The priest is chanting 'Be my Guide and Light, Saint Mary, Holy Virgin'. The inscription around the tomb reads: 'Richard de Wotton, born in this village, and most appropriately taking his name from it, lies here: from whom the Virgin Mary, holy and most beautiful, receives – as was her wish – the gift of masses'. From the richness of the memorial it is believed that Richard was probably a founder of the church.

Last of the church's great possessions is the organ, in the S aisle. It was constructed around 1720 by Christopher Schrider, who followed in the footsteps of his master, and later father-in-law, the German 'Father Smith', as a craftsman organ-maker. It was presented by George I to St Martin-in-the-Fields, London, a church of which he was at one time warden. At the opening ceremony it was played by Handel, a favourite of the King; Handel was so impressed with the organ that he returned often to play it. Over the years, however, it became dilapidated owing to poor maintenance, and was put up for sale in 1799, it being thought that repair was not worth while. It was bought in 1800 and installed in Wotton. It was renovated in 1837, but about three-quarters of the pipework is Schrider's, and the oak case also original.

If the interior of the church is a collection of well-cared-for treasures, the churchyard itself has not had such a happy history. In 1783 the vicar noted that it was 'more like a dunghill or tip for rubbish and filth . . . the graves are so shallow that if horses got in they often broke the coffins'. Eventually the complaints were so frequent that the cemetery was closed, a new one being opened in 1921.

Leave Wotton by the strangely named Sinwell Lane and then go up
Lisleway Hill, until a track R (W) is signposted, 'Tor Hill 1·5 km,
Wortley 3 km, Alderley 4 km'. This track, part metalled, part mud,
leads out to yet more superb viewing points, an arc around the scarp
with views out to the southern end of the Vale of Berkeley and
beyond to the Mendips. Make the most of this view. Apart from
that at the Somerset monument, visible ahead, and a more limited
one at Old Sodbury church, it is the last, as the scarp dies away.
From here the country changes, with gentle wooded valleys and
'soft' downland country replacing the bold scarp scenery. Originally
the area from here southwards was known as the South Wolds,
which recognised the change of character, but the distinction has
long since been lost.

After following the scarp around, the Way descends a flank of
Wortley Hill and skirts Wortley village to the country beyond.
Wortley itself is another '-ley' village: the Wyrt Leah, the clearing
for vegetable growing. It was also the birthplace of Stephen
Hopkins, a local clothier who sailed in the *Mayflower* with the
Pilgrim Fathers in 1620. That trip was his second to the New World,
his previous one having ended in disaster with a mutiny, in which he
played a part, and a shipwreck off Bermuda. As the Jamestown
colony was starving when he eventually reached it, he returned to
London. Hopkins had been educated at Wotton, where he also
learnt the wool trade. He obviously learnt it well because he made a
fortune in London, travelling in the *Mayflower* with two
menservants. In America he was Miles Standish's right-hand man
and eventually became a high-ranking official. He died in 1644.
Wortley also has a fine example of a Georgian mansion built around
1707 by the Osborne family, local mill owners. Although the house
is attached to an older building, it is the Georgian section that
attracts the interest, particularly the interior where there is a square
stairwell with an elegant oak staircase lit by a 10-ft-square Venetian
window containing much of the original green glass.

Though tiny, Wortley played an important part in the early
prosperity of the area because of its closeness to the stream

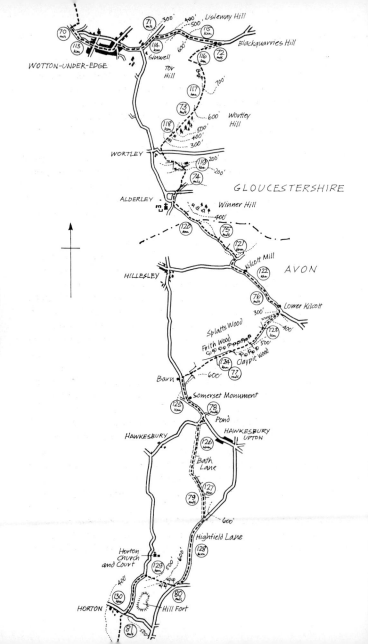

descending from Ozleworth Bottom to Michaelwood. The 5-mile length around Wortley had no less than 15 mills, many of them of good size. In addition, there were the dozen or more around Wotton, those around Kingswood, and still more on the Kilcott tributary, nearly all of them cloth mills, a remarkably heavy concentration. OS Sheet ST79 shows five disused mills in the mile length of the stream centred on Wortley even now.

Beyond Wortley the Way crosses fields to emerge at the bottom of a lane leading up to Alderley. This lane has a spring near where the Way joins it that causes the lower section to be more stream than lane. The spring, with water emerging over a moss-laden stone parapet, is very picturesque. At the top of the lane the Way enters Alderley.

Alderley, 'Alar Leah' – the clearing in the alders – is a lovely village, delightfully picturesque. It is a quiet place, but has had its moments of fame. In the 16c it was famous for its fossils – 'stones clearly fascioned lyke cokills and myghty shells of great oysters turned into stones'. The following century saw the birth of Matthew Hale, later Lord Chief Justice, perhaps Alderley's most famous son. He was born here in 1609 and found fame as a man of honesty in corrupt times, when to be honest at all was an achievement of merit. He was extremely religious, claiming not to have missed church for more than 30 years, and was reputedly kind and gentle. These qualities did not extend to the Bench, however, where he is known to have condemned a woman to death for witchcraft. He certainly believed in witches, claiming that they were proved by 'the Scriptures, laws of all nations and by the wisdom of Parliament'. He died in Alderley in 1676 two years before the publication of his 'Pleas for the crown', a 'brief and inaccurate digest of criminal law'. He is buried in the churchyard along with others of the Hale family in a small plot fenced off from the rest of the yard.

The church itself is interesting. Though the tower is 15c, the main body was built in 1806, one of very few actually constructed, as opposed to renovated, at this time. This main body is free of arcades dividing aisles from nave, and has a painted ceiling in imitation of fan-vaulting. There is also some fine oak carving, particularly on the pulpit.

The churchyard, as already noted, contains Hale family tombs, and many other tombs besides. For the most part they are much weathered and badly obscured, but there are some interesting mouldings including one headstone with an egg-timer and bible. Immediately outside the door is a table tomb with an interesting inscription that can just be read before it disappears into the grass – 'John Stanton – minister who after his exile for religion began to preach the gospel of Christ in this parish in 1558'. He died in 1572. The year he began to preach was the first of Queen Elizabeth's reign and the start of the new Reformation, with a proclamation that the Gospels be read in English.

Next to the church is Alderley House, an Elizabethan mansion with clustered chimneys and excellent windows. It was the seat of the lord of the manor, but is now a preparatory school for boys.

A curious link with the north Cotswolds is the presence in the village of a St Kenelm's Spring and a St Kenelm's Lane. Why the name should be used here is a mystery. Mystery also surrounds an incident reputed to have taken place in Alderley in 1225. It appears that a local inhabitant decided one day that he was the reincarnation of Jesus Christ. Unimpressed, the local magistrates had him taken to Oxford, where he was executed. The story was not written down until 1550, when it was said that the execution was by crucifixion.

The Way leaves Alderley by turning along the front of an elegant green house and on past a barn on staddle stones, a reminder that this is still Wold country. From then on, follow the right-hand hedge of the field that slopes down from Foxholes Wood, passing a superb, conical holly tree and going through a gate and down to the R of a lonely dead tree. On this path the Way passes from Gloucestershire into the new county of Avon. The track here, by the double gate and stile, can be very muddy in wet weather and spirits are not improved by reaching a lane with a marker post having a faded blue arrow pointing L and a brighter yellow one pointing R. The yellow is the Cotswold Way marker. Go down to the Kilcott road, which is really little more than a lane, despite its tarmac. In spring, with the hedgerows budding and the stream flowing gently down the very edge of the road, this lane is good walking, tarmac or not. The derivation of the name Kilcott is disputed. It could be from 'Cylla Cot', the cottage of Cylla, or from 'Kil-y-coed', the wooded valley. Certainly the latter still stands as a descriptive name for the valley.

Kilcott Mill is passed, one of several on the Kilcott stream that helped the general prosperity of the area. Here there is still a large millpond, proverbially calm. The Way continues on along the lane until the hamlet of Lower Kilcott is reached. Turn R (SW), uphill, at a sign 'Hawkesbury Monument 2·5, Hawkesbury 3 km', the *second* sign with the same distances that the walker comes to.

Go up steeply and then follow an obvious, if indistinct, track to Claypit Wood. From the end of the wood go across the field to a gate-less gateway and then head for the barn on the horizon. This barn is on the opposite side of a minor road that is followed to the Hawkesbury Monument. The monument itself can be glimpsed

Kilcott: The mill and mill pond

Hawkesbury Upton: The Somerset Monument

occasionally through the trees to the L of the route from Claypit
Wood, acting as a beacon to the walker. The monument was erected
in 1846 to the memory of General Lord Robert Edward Henry
Somerset, which explains the alternative name of Somerset
Monument. General Somerset was a member of the Beaufort family
whose seat is at nearby Badminton. He served under Wellington and
was commended by Parliament for his enthusiasm at the battle of
Waterloo. For a small fee the walker can climb the tower, giving the
last panoramic views from the high scarp on a southern transit of
the Cotswold Way.

The Way then carries on down the road into Hawkesbury Upton.
'Upton' is from 'Upp Tun', the upper farm, distinguishing the
village here from that of Hawkesbury in the valley 250 ft below.
'Hawkesbury' is derived from 'Hafoc's Burh', Hafoc's camp. There
is no evidence of a fort near by, so the name is presumably derived
from a less specific camp, perhaps just a defended dwelling. The
Way does not enter the village, the route going R to meet Bath Lane
at the pond. Bath Lane can be quite muddy in wet weather, but
gives pleasant views out over the Severn Vale before it meets
Highfield Lane. This is followed to its junction with Bodkin Hazel
Lane, where the Way leads off to the R, down through woodland to
the first half of Horton village, the church and Court.

Description of route continues on p. 195.

3 The South Wolds

Horton: The 14c church of St James

Horton is another village whose name derivation is the subject of discussion. It could be 'Heorot Dun', the hill of stags, or 'Horo Tun', the town in the mud.

Horton Court is open to the public between April and the end of October on Wednesdays and Saturdays, 2–6 pm, being administered by the National Trust. It has a considerable claim to being the oldest inhabited house in England as well as in the Cotswolds, the hall being the remains of a Norman house built in the first half of the 12c. The Norman Robert de Tedini was granted the manor after it was confiscated from the Saxon lord Ulf, a son of King Harold. Ulf escaped death at Hastings, possibly by not being there, but refused to acknowledge William and was banished to Normandy and obscurity. The house built at Horton was domestic and unfortified, one of very few known. The hall is all that now remains of the house, and its roof is 14c. The principal remaining Norman works are the N and S doorways, even the windows having been replaced some 200 years after the original construction. It seems likely that the reason for the major renovation work in the 14c was that excess thrust by the original roof had caused the walls to bow outwards. Inside the hall there is a small museum containing articles not connected with it. There is a collection of pewter on a table constructed from a single huge tree, which has only four legs despite its length. There is also a collection of armour of the Civil War period and some bicycles, including a penny-farthing.

The Tudor Gothic Court itself was added to the hall around 1520 by Dr William Knight, who held the prebend or canonship of Horton. Knight is an interesting figure, another who rose from lowly beginnings to high distinction under Henry VIII. His doctorate was in law, and he was for a time Henry's chief secretary. He was an eminent churchman, with positions in the cathedrals of Lincoln, Bangor and Salisbury, and was such a brilliant diplomat that he was appointed prothonotary and sent to Rome in 1527 to negotiate with the Pope for Henry's divorce from Katherine of Aragon. Being proud of his hard-earnt distinction, he placed the coat of arms that he had been granted over the main door of the Court, as well as over a fireplace. Above the coat of arms is the prothonotary hat.

Knight also built the loggia, or ambulatory, in the garden. Many gardens of that period had similar covered walks, but usually they were cloister-like, being rather closer to the main body of the house. It is possible that Knight had in mind the Italian loggia style, a possibility made more likely by the inclusion of the four medallions of Roman emperors on the back wall. The building is shadowed by a superb tulip tree, reputedly the largest in England.

From the Court, the church is reached by a short walk through the gardens. Note, as you walk, the numerous bronze and stone statuettes of figures in what are perhaps best described as artistic poses.

The church is of basic 14c construction, though it was much modified in the 15c and 16c. In the porch, look for the figure of the man with bagpipes on one of the supporting columns. Inside the church, the nave is separated from the N aisle by a 14c arcade to the W end of which is a gargoyle-like figure of a man with his tongue sticking out. Look also for the memorial to Anne Paston in the chapel at the end of the N aisle. She was married to John Paston, whose family had owned the manor since 1552, and died in 1731. After lauding her as a 'most loving wife, a tender Mother, a faithful Friend' it notes that she died 'by a most tedious and painful sickness, suffered with the greatest Courage and Patience'. Even allowing for the proviso on courage it is unusual to see death referred to in such honest terms.

On leaving the church, look at the clock on the S side of the tower. It fell apart in 1733 and now only the handless face is left. Moreover the bells in the tower are no longer rung because they are not thought safe.

Horton: The Court. The 12c Norman hall is to the L (above). The Court ambulatory (below)

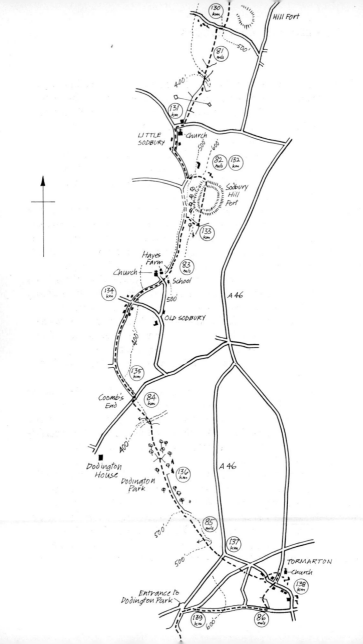

Hill Fort

130 km

81 mls

500'

400'

131 km

LITTLE SODBURY

Church

500

600

82 mls   132 km

Sodbury Hill Fort

133 km

Hayes Farm

Church

83 mls

School

134 km

500

A 46

OLD SODBURY

400

135 km

Coomb's End

84 km

400

Dodington House

Dodington Park

136 km

A 46

500

85 mls

137 km

TORMARTON

Church

138 km

Entrance to Dodington Park

139 km

600

86 mls

The Way now continues S to the other half of the village built after the construction of the 'main' road. It then goes across country to Little Sodbury, which it enters between a cottage on the R and its garden on the L. Northbound walkers can find this easily, the cottage being the last of the row.

Following the road around L at the triangle brings the walker to Little Sodbury church. The church is unique in England in its dedication to St Adeline. Originally the church stood behind the manor but it was in such a poor state that in 1859 it was demolished. The work was carried out carefully, and the stones were used to assist the rebuilding on the present site, closer to the village. The church was built to the same plan as the original, except that it was not given a flat roof. The original manor church was dedicated to St Adeline, the patron saint of Flemish weavers. This again suggests the theory that the expertise of the Cotswold wool trade was based on Flemish master craftsmen. In the vicinity of Little Sodbury there are villages with Flemish names: Dunkirk, Petty France. Internally the church is neat but contains little from the time when William Tyndale preached in it, in its original situation. The pulpit is interesting, containing five panels with figures of Hooper, Latimer, Ridley, Cranmer and Tyndale, who were all martyred at the time of the Reformation.

Up the hill from the church is the manor house that is the focus of Little Sodbury. The manor had an unremarkable line of lords following the dispossession of the Saxon Aluward after the Norman Conquest, until it passed to John Walsh in the late 15c. He probably fought with Henry Richmond, later Henry VII, at the battle of Bosworth, thus obtaining the favour of Henry, which assisted his son, Sir John Walsh, to obtain high office. Sir John was twice High Sheriff of Gloucestershire, and acted as King's Champion at the coronation of Henry VIII in 1509. Later he was host to Henry and Anne Boleyn who stayed for a few days, probably in the Oriel room, the name given to the room overlooking the Severn Vale that contains an oriel window. With Sir John's death in 1547 the manor passed to Maurice Walsh. One summer day in 1556 when Maurice and seven of his children were sitting at dinner during a severe thunderstorm a 'sulphureous globe' came into the room through the open door, traversed it and passed out through a window opposite. One child was killed instantly and four others were so badly injured that they died soon after. By September Maurice was also dead, apparently as a result of the same incident. This sounds like an example of the much-discussed ball lightning.

After the Walshes the manor had another uneventful period, the house itself falling into disrepair at the beginning of this century when it was bought by the Beaufort family and restored.

The earliest building was erected in the middle of the 15c by the Stanshaw family that preceded the Walshes. Some of this still remains, notably the W porch and the great hall. The great hall is considered to be one of the finest examples of its type and has hardly been altered since its construction. The open-timbered ceiling is particularly good. The house was added to and altered by the Walshes, the dining-room being the best example of this Tudor period. Since that time there have been additions and renovations, but the basic character of the house has been retained.

The house is a private dwelling, but the present owners are willing to show visitors around, provided sufficient notice is given so that a suitable time can be arranged.

Many visitors are anxious to see the attic that is traditionally known as Tyndale's Room. Despite his fame it is not known where or when William Tyndale was born. The Tyndales were well established in Gloucestershire, with branches at Stinchcombe, North Nibley, Cam and Slimbridge, the latter being the favoured birthplace. All that is known of his date of birth is that it was between 1490 and 1495. This date is arrived at by working backwards from 1515 when he received his MA at Oxford and was ordained. Tyndale then went to Cambridge and was probably present at the public burning of Martin Luther's books following his excommunication in 1520.

He moved to Little Sodbury Manor in 1521 to join Sir John Walsh's household. It is not clear what precise position he held; probably he acted as tutor to the children, secretary to Sir John and chaplain to the household. In the latter capacity he used the original

St Adeline's church that stood behind the manor house. All that
now remains above ground of that church is a doorway and a small
section of wall. Beside the doorway still stand the original yew trees.
It seems that Tyndale's time at Little Sodbury was crucial to his
eventual life's work. Certainly by then he had decided that the
typical clergyman of the day was more interested in his social
position than in promoting the Christian ethic by teaching. This
view was supported by the condition of the peasants, many of whom
Tyndale must have seen in his walks in the area. For the most part
they were hard-working, but underfed and desperately poor. They
were also superstitious, which Tyndale saw as due to a lack of
positive guidance. It was at a dinner in the manor house that he
made his famous remark to a visiting high dignitary. In an enraged
attempt to silence the scripture-quoting upstart, the dignitary
shouted 'We were better be without God's law than the Pope's', to
which Tyndale replied: 'I defy the Pope and all his laws. If God
shall spare my life, ere many years I will cause the boy that follows
the plough to know more of the Bible than thou doest.' It has been
speculated that the recipient of this caustic repartee was Dr William
Knight of Horton Court. Remarks like this one, coupled with an
intimate knowledge of the Scriptures to back his arguments, and
some of the sermons he preached in nearby rooms, villages and in
the open air on College Green, Bristol, made Tyndale many enemies
and also made his presence at the manor house an embarrassment to
Walsh. Finally in 1523 he left to go to London. The parting seems to
have been amicable, with reluctance on both sides. Certainly Walsh
gave him a letter of introduction to people in London. It is possible
that the move was based solely on the need for Tyndale to continue
his work of translating the Bible without implicating friends. While
at the manor house he had already translated some of the works of
Erasmus. It seems he quickly became disillusioned in London and in
1524 he went to Hamburg. Here he continued his translation, and in
1526 his English New Testament was printed at Worms. Only two
copies now exist of this printing, one in the library of St Paul's,
London, the other at the Baptist College in Bristol.

Tyndale began a translation of the Old Testament, assisted, at
Antwerp, in 1530, by Miles Coverdale, whom we have already met

at Sudeley Castle. By this time the climate in England was changing.
Henry VIII spoke favourably of him, and by 1534 he was himself
being petitioned by the clergy of Canterbury to allow an English
Bible. But though times were changing they did not change fast
enough, and in May 1535 Tyndale was betrayed by Henry Phillips,
probably acting on orders from England. He was imprisoned,
charged with heresy, tried and found guilty. On 6 October 1536 his
body was burnt at the stake in the courtyard of the castle of
Vilvorde after he had been executed by strangulation.

Within two years the change in England was complete, Henry VIII
decreeing, in 1538, that every church in England should have an
English Bible. He gave permission for two translations, one by Miles
Coverdale and the other by John Rogers under the name of Thomas
Matthew. Although Tyndale's name is in neither, most of each of
the translations is his work.

From the manor house, the waymarking is a little ambiguous. The
Way goes uphill to the barns on the top and past them to reach
Sodbury Hill Fort beyond. This camp, probably the finest
multivallate fort on the Cotswold Edge, is rectangular and encloses
about 11 acres. The W side depends for defence on the scarp edge;
on the other three sides there are double ramparts with ditches
separated by a wide berm. The ditches have silted up, and the
original stone ramparts have been eroded and covered over, but
nevertheless they are still awesome, 12 ft high and 8 ft deep. To walk
along the ditch and look up at the rampart is to gain some idea of
the colossal work that must have gone into the construction.

The camp has seen considerable service over the years. It is
basically Iron Age, but was almost certainly strengthened and used
by the Romans as one of their frontier posts. Then, in 577, the
Saxon army camped here before moving on to the fateful battle of
Dyrham. There was a battle near here around 930 when King
Athelstan routed a large band of marauders. Later still, in 1471,
Edward IV and his brother, Richard, later Richard III, rested their
army here before moving off through the darkness of the early
morning of 3 May 1471 to the battle of Tewkesbury where the army
of Margaret of Anjou was destroyed and her son killed.

Leave the camp by the obvious break in the southern rampart and go on to the gate, which has a confusion of arrows. Follow the ones with the dots above them to descend the (W) scarp edge and then traverse back S at about half height, to the village of Old Sodbury.

Old Sodbury, together with nearby Chipping Sodbury, formed a manor that was separate from Little Sodbury at the time of the Norman Conquest. The name is derived from 'Soppa Burh', Soppa's fort. At the time of the Norman Conquest the manor was owned by Brictric, a powerful Saxon thane. He had been in Normandy before 1066 on a mission for Edward the Confessor, and while there had 'found great favour' with Matilda, the 15-year-old daughter of the high-ranking Count Baldwin. Brictric made it quite clear that he had no intention of marrying her, and returned home. Unfortunately for him, Matilda married William, who became the Conqueror, and when she arrived in England she proved that she was possessed of a long memory and a vengeful spirit. Brictric was dispossessed of his lands – Matilda taking them personally – and thrown into prison. He spent at least 14 years in prison, some stories saying he was released when Matilda died in 1080. Other versions maintain he died in prison.

The Way emerges into Old Sodbury at the village school, and a little to the R from here is the parish church. It is likely that the village had a church as early as 783, and it is also likely that it stood on this spot, the Saxons liking to put their churches on knolls. The current church was constructed in the early 13c, though little of it is original, the body of the church having been rebuilt, but faithfully so, in the mid-19c. The tower is original, as is the inner S door, which is a particularly good example of the late Norman style. Note the beautifully preserved carving. Internally the church is neat and quiet. The chancel has a fine wooden arched ceiling differing from that of the nave, which is of more usual design.

In the N transept, there are two effigies, one in stone, the other in oak, that have not been satisfactorily dated or identified. Each is life-size and represents a knight, in chain mail, with legs crossed. From the similarity of the stone effigy with that of Robert de Bitton in Bitton church, dated 1225, it is believed to be a Knight Templar of the early 13c. The wooden effigy is rarer; the only other surviving specimen in the country is in Gloucester Cathedral, and is believed to be later, possibly late 13c. Identification is not possible, although it has been suggested that the effigies could represent members of the de Sodbury family that resided locally at that time; or that they could be Jordano Bissop, lord of the manor of Little Sodbury, who died in 1278, and his son Sir John. Since Little Sodbury church has never possessed a churchyard, its burials have always taken place at Old Sodbury.

The church also contains a memorial to David Hartly, who lived at Little Sodbury Manor and, as 'envoy extraordinary and plenipotentiary to the Court of Versailles', negotiated the peace settlement with America in 1783.

Externally the church has some interesting features. The E window is very fine and has two excellent carved heads of a prelate and a king. Beneath it is a curious T-shaped stone inscribed with four curious floral cross motifs. There is no known explanation for this stone, and it is thought that it may have come already inscribed from another site, possibly a Roman villa. In the churchyard beside the E wall is a magnificent horse-chestnut. From the iron gate at the W end of the church there is a good view out over the lower Severn Vale.

From the church, the Way goes on down Cotswold Lane to the main A432. Cross this with care and continue along Chapel Lane to Coomb's End, where the Way enters Dodington Park. To the SW of the Way's entrance to the Park is an official entrance to the house and the additional features common to open stately homes. The house is the ancestral home of the Codrington family, which first achieved note when John Codrington fought with bravery at Agincourt. In recognition of his services he was appointed the King's standard bearer. Later the family split over allegiance to King or Parliament during the Civil War, another John choosing the King's side, while his brother Robert chose Parliament. The making of the family fortunes occurred around this time when another brother, Christopher, left to carve a fortune from the West Indian jungle. By the end of the 18c, the family, of which another Christopher was then head, was immensely rich, even by the standards of the day. Their fortune was, as were all those made in the West Indies, based on slavery, and Codrington bitterly opposed abolition. Today it is difficult to feel sympathy with such a position, or with the man taking it, but it must be said in fairness, that the Codringtons appear to have been relatively enlightened, caring for the welfare of their slaves and allowing them a measure of independence and responsibility.

The park as we see it is due, in large part, to that 18c genius Capability Brown, who landscaped it around 1760 for Sir William Codrington. He transformed the original park with controlled addition and removal of tree clumps, and the digging of lakes. Later, around 1800, the original Tudor house was demolished by Christopher Codrington, who employed James Wyatt as architect of

Dodington House

the present house, which took 20 years to build. It seems that Wyatt wished to avoid the prevalent Palladian style and produce something simple, even severe, but Codrington demanded some adhesion to the classical style. The result is relatively harmonious though the massive Corinthian columns of the W front seem a little heavy. Detailed accounts remain for the house. They show that up to 1811 the building cost was £58,613. 13. 0½d., at a time when a good farm worker could earn £12 per year.

Internally the house is a minor treasure-house of furniture, paintings and curios. It also contains in the central stairway one of Wyatt's finest works, a masterpiece in its use of space. The ironwork on the stairs seems dated now, but it must be remembered that in its day it was a novel feature.

Apart from the house, there are museums of coaches and coaching equipment, and of antique agricultural implements. The house and gardens are open between Easter and September from 11.00 a.m. until 5.30 p.m.

The route through the park is relatively easy to follow if you remember to go SE. There are no Cotswold Way markers, but there are huge white 'Public Footpath' signs on trees at stategic places. From the last sign the route drops into a gentle valley, crosses the stream by a bridge and then heads for the obvious break in the wall on the horizon. This break is a gate to the A46. From there, a series of fields, stiles and short road hops leads to Tormarton village.

Description of route continues on p. 207.

Tormarton

Anciently, the village stood at the boundary between Wessex and
Mercia, the second part of the name being from 'macre tun', the
farm on the boundary. The prefix 'tor' is disputed. It could be from
'torr', a hill, though this is topographically unlikely; 'Thor', the god;
or a mutation of 'thorn', a thorn tree. Because of its situation, away
from the main A46 road, the village has, to a certain extent, escaped
the modernisation of many in the South Wolds, and remains a quiet
and secluded place of considerable charm. There is an old story of
the time when the village had a large pond at the E end. It was felt
by the villagers that the continuous rains that swept in from the E
were due to the pond, and consequently it was filled in.

There was a priest at the time of Domesday, implying the
existence of a Saxon church, an implication strengthened by the
Saxon stones to be found in the tower of the present church. This
is basically late Norman, though there has been much rebuilding
since. Of the Norman features, especially noteworthy are the external
string-courses, raised horizontal bands, on the E chancel wall.
Though cut into by the E window, they are still well preserved. The
lower of the two is a common Norman feature, but the upper one is
of a design known as 'wheat-ear', the only other known example in
England being at Norwich Cathedral.

The church is entered through an external arch that has a fine pair
of carved heads. Internally the interest lies mainly in the memorials,
though the Jacobean pulpit is good and the pews near the door
marked 'Free' are a reminder of times gone by. Chief amongst the
memorials is the brass to John Ceysill in the floor of the nave
beneath the carpet. Ceysill was 'famulus', probably steward, to Sir
John St Loe, or Sendlow, the rector of Tormarton. The Latin-
inscribed plaque gives the date of his death as 1493, on the Eve of St
Bartholomew, 23 August. The brass is very good, particularly in its
fine detail, for instance the pen and inkhorn at Ceysill's waist. Those
wishing to make a rubbing are asked to read the notice displayed in
the church.

If the Ceysill memorial is the best in the church, the oldest is that
which, paradoxically, does not exist. In the floor of the chancel is

the matrix of a brass of Sir John de la Rivere. The brass is long gone but the outline shows a floriated cross within the head of which the knight stands holding in his hand a model of the church. This should not be taken, as it usually is, to mean that Sir John was founder of the church. It was already ancient when the memorial was inset around 1350. It is likely, though, that he was a benefactor, possibly contributing greatly to a major rebuilding programme.

The other memorial of note is that to Edward Topp, who held the manor until his death in 1699. It is to be found behind the organ. Above the inscription is a painted relief of Topp's coat of arms consisting of a grey mailed fist clutching a pink arm which has been severed, the soggy end depicted in gory red.

In the churchyard near the N wall a little E of the church itself is an ancient headstone with a motif looking remarkably similar to those on the E wall of Old Sodbury church.

Tormarton: The timbered roof of St Mary Magdalene (above) and the memorial brass to John Ceysill, St Mary Magdalene Church (left)

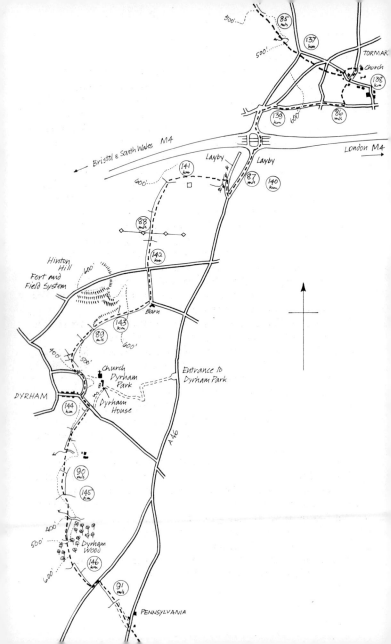

Tormarton to Dyrham

The Way leaves Tormarton by a path beside the village shop and
then follows a minor road to the A46. Go S, passing another
entrance to Dodington Park, to reach the M4 motorway. Cross the
motorway roundabout with care, follow the A46 to the second lay-
by, and cross to the wood behind it. From the wood the Way is easily
followed to Hinton Hill, a little N of Dyrham. The hill is remarkable
for the clarity with which the ancient strip-lynchet field system is
seen. The lynchets, literally low banks, were terraced slopes for
cultivation purposes and may be either Saxon or medieval in origin.
Above the system is the remains of a hill fort which saw a decisive
battle in the struggle for supremacy in this area. There is no
monument to the battle and yet in its way this place is at the
crossroads of the history of this country. The Anglo-Saxon
Chronicle states that in 577 'Cuthwine and Ceawlin fought against
the Britons and killed three kings, Conmail, Condidan and
Farinmail, at the place called Dyrham, and they captured three of
their cities, Gloucester, Cirencester and Bath (Akeman)'. Behind this
simple sentence lie events that shaped England.

   The Saxons had been pushing W for many years across the downs
of Berkshire and Wiltshire and also in the S, with the aim of
attacking Bath. The southern group was led by Ceawlin, King of the
West Saxons, or of Wessex, as it became known. The decisive time
came when his army cut the Cirencester-Bath road and camped in
the fort of Hinton Hill. Deprived of a strong defence based on a
single city, the Britons decided to attack, but had the problem of
manoeuvring their two northern and single southern armies into
position. It is likely that their efforts to keep the separate armies out
of the reach of the Saxons, whose job would have been made easy
by fighting them one at a time, led to the British being tired and
dispirited when the battle came. They also made the tactical mistake
of attacking a well-defended enemy, the push up the hill being
hopeless from the start. There are no details of the battle, other than
that the Saxons won, with the gain of the strategic Severn Vale. The
stage had been set for the country to become English, and for the
British to retreat, to Wales and Cornwall.

   The Way now moves easily on to the more peaceful delights of
Dyrham, a village of charm with a fine church.

Dyrham: The Russel brass in St Peter's Church

Dyrham

The church is at the end of a short lane that starts from the road
and opposite which, behind the wall, are magnificent rhododendron
bushes. The church itself is of interest more for its setting than for
any great architectural merit. It does, however, contain some fine
memorials including the Russel brass which, as mentioned before, is
believed to be contemporary with the Berkeley brass in Wotton-
under-Edge. The brass portrays Sir Maurice Russel and his wife,
Isobel. Sir Maurice, who died in 1401, was a lord of the manor who
rebuilt the church in the late 14c. A translation of the Latin
inscription on the brass reads

> Entombed here, bereft of life,
> Behold a gentle knight!
> Beneath this stone he lieth prone
> Once Morys Russel Knight,
> And Isobel his loving spouse.
> In marble rare enclosed,
> Hidden from sight of earthly wight,
> Hath here her limbs reposed.
> The joy of Heaven bestow on these
> Blest Trinity of grace:
> Past, present, future – Death shall seize
> Who are of mortal race.

The brass is superb, and the similarity between the pose of Lady
Isobel, and that of Margaret, Lady Berkeley is striking.

Another interesting memorial is that to George Wynter at the end
of the S aisle. It is an imposing work, with a canopy supported by
stone columns, the whole finely sculptured. Wynter was another lord
of the manor, who died in 1581, and lies, in stone, on the tomb with
his wife surrounded by his eleven children, their hands clasped in
prayer. One of the four sons depicted is John Wynter, who
commanded the *Elizabeth*, a ship that sailed with Drake's *Golden
Hind*. After passing through the Magellan Straits, Wynter's ship
became separated from Drake's and, against the wishes of his crew,
Wynter turned back to arrive in Ilfracombe in 1579. Since Drake

went on to circle the world, Dyrham came within an ace of having a famous son.

The church is also possessed of a fine series of hatchments, the coats of arms hung over the doors of deceased persons during the period of mourning. A sheet in the church describes the series.

Immediately beside the church is Dyrham House, standing in a huge open park. Members of the National Trust may enter from the churchyard itself, but others must use the entrance on the A46 some ¾ mile away.

The house and gardens, administered by the National Trust, are worth a visit. The house was built by William Blathwayt who married Mary Wynter, the great-great-grand-daughter of George Wynter, whose noble tomb is in the church. Blathwayt was a very able civil servant, fluent in Dutch, who was Secretary of War under William III. He married Mary Wynter in late 1686, when she was 36,

Dyrham: The House from the E

but she died in November 1691 after, or perhaps because of, having had 4 children. Following her death, he transformed the grounds and demolished the original Tudor house. He then constructed the present house, which is an excellent example of baroque planning. He was assisted in the work by an unknown French architect, Samuel Hauduroy. At the centre of the house is a great hall that is believed to be the last remnant of the original Tudor house. Grouped around it are a variety of rooms, many of which are elegantly panelled, containing a number of paintings by minor artists. The walnut staircase is a good example of the style of the late 17c.

The E front, which is quite imposing when seen from the high ground of the park, is by a different architect, William Talman, an assistant to Sir Christopher Wren. It is typical of the late English baroque period, and its bold rectangular shape is pleasing even if the whole is a little over-elaborate.

The grounds are now a deer park containing a herd of the rare fallow deer. The usage is by no means new, since the name Dyrham derives from 'Deor Hamm', deer enclosure. In their original form the grounds contained the most ambitious water gardens in Britain. There was a dammed lake feeding fountains on long terraces, a cascade of 224 steps and a 20-ft water jet that was reputedly the finest piece of hydraulic engineering in the country. By the late 18c, the water gardens were in an advanced state of decay and today only the long-dry Neptune fountain, carved by John Harvey of Bath, remains.

Dyrham House is open from 2–6 p.m. in June to September every day except Friday, and 2–6 p.m. in April, May and October every day except Thursday and Friday.

Dyrham Park is open all year from 12–6 p.m. or dusk.

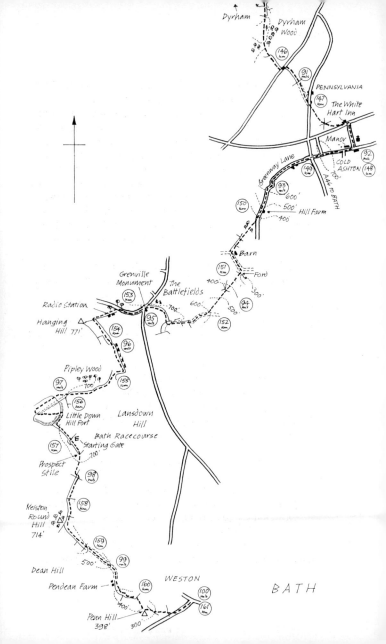

The Way leaves Dyrham by going R (S) off the road at the road sign announcing the village. A path across country leads to the disappointing remains of Dyrham Wood, beyond which a lane leads down to the hamlet of Pennsylvania. There is no obvious reason for the name in this situation. The Way leads on to Cold Ashton, the first name of which was added because of its exposed position. Ashton is derived either from 'Aesc Tun', the farm near the ash trees, or from 'Aesca Tun', the farm near the water. The latter is not as unlikely as might first appear since there are many springs near the village forming a stream that, at one time, fed Bath. The village is reached easily and the Way actually goes through the yard of its interesting church, reaching it by following the path opposite the White Hart Inn.

The church was largely rebuilt in the early 16c, though the style used has similarities to 14c work, in keeping with the tower which is of that age. The rebuilding was carried out at the expense of Thomas Key who was rector at that time, though how he had obtained the money for such a grand project is not known. The church has, in several places, the device used by Key, the letter T and a key entwined. Look, for instance, at the outer doorway and at the glass in the chantry E window.

Inside the church are some rare treasures. The oak pulpit, which has been restored, still contains some superb early 16c panels and stands beneath an equally good, richly ornate canopy. Beside this is a stairway that led to a gallery, a supporting corbel for which can still be seen on the wall opposite. The stairway can be followed to the old doorway.

Near the pulpit, carefully kept in a glass case, is an original Authorised Version of the Bible from 1611.

The Latin epitaph to Thomas Key, translated, reads: 'Buried in ground thereby made famous lies the worshipped Thomas surnamed Key, Rector, who, of his love of God Almighty, did at his own cost build all this holy church. May God, Most Holy, Three in One, for such a gift grant him a place in His Heavenly Kingdom'.

The church also contains a very good example of the hagioscope,

or squint, in this case from the chantry to the chancel. Squints were
included to allow the congregation in the chantry to see the priest at
the altar. Other churches on the route have examples of such
squints, particularly Painswick, which has a double one, but rarely
are they more obvious.

Leaving the church, the Way continues to the older part of the
village, entering it opposite a beautiful old cottage with an old water
pump in the garden. The route goes R (W) from here and passes
Cold Ashton Manor. The manor is Elizabethan and has been called
the most perfect house of its time in England. The manor, and the
original house, were owned by Bath Abbey which lost it at the
Dissolution when it passed to the well-established Denys family.
They sold it to William Pepwall, a wealthy Bristol merchant who
was also mayor of Bristol. It is likely that the present house was
commenced by him in the late 16c, although work was also carried

Cold Ashton: The Manor House

out by John Gunning, who bought it from the Pepwalls, in the early
17c. Gunning was also a mayor of Bristol and it is his coat of arms
over the stone gateway. The house was restored at a later stage of its
life but great care was taken not to alter the essential character and
the house remains a fine example of Elizabethan architecture. Note
particularly the excellent doorway.

Despite its beauty, the manor has not always seen life at its best.
Following the battle of Lansdown, Sir Bevil Granville was brought
to the village, and in the manor (or, less likely, the rectory), he died
of his wounds. The Way now reverses the route taken by the dying
leader by going down to the A46 and crossing into Greenway Lane.
Follow it as it goes steeply into the valley and as it levels out and
goes L take a footpath R (SW) into a small, and invariably
waterlogged, copse. From the wood the route is not well marked,
but goes across several fields towards a distant barn. At the barn go
L (S), down and over the cattle grid, and then strike out R (SW)
across the fields, climbing steeply through them to a track beyond.
Where the track ends, go across to the Granville Monument.

The Monument and the local area, still known as The Battlefields,
commemorate the battle of Lansdown fought on 5 July 1643. The
battle was fought because Sir William Waller, the Parliamentarian
governor of Bath, was attempting to forestall an attack on the city
by the combined Royalist armies of Sir Ralph Hopton, Prince
Maurice and the Marquis of Hertford which had joined each other
at Chewton Mendip. Being a good General, Waller took up a position
on the northern tip of Lansdown, dominating the steep slope, and
built earthworks behind which he mounted cannons. He then fought
the Royalist armies at the base of the hill, perhaps hoping to use the
cannon on the spur to fire into the Royalists after a mock retreat, or
perhaps having made a miscalculation. Whichever is true, the result
was the same, the Parliamentarians retreating up the slope pursued
by Royalists who were heavily bombarded by the cannon. At this
point Sir Bevil Granville led his Cornishmen in a storming of the hill
in an attempt to silence the guns. Granville was an inspiration to his
men, riding back and forth across the hill until he was unhorsed and
then pole-axed. The blow fell at his moment of triumph, his men
winning through and forcing Waller's men to retreat to the shelter

of stone walls some 400 yards away. The Royalists, tired and battle-weary and, no doubt, demoralised by the loss of Granville, did not press home the attack but settled down to wait out the night.

Through the night the Royalists watched the lights flicker in Waller's camp and in the morning they stormed the wall. At the wall they discovered that Waller had quietly withdrawn his troops to Bath during the night, leaving slow-burning cords behind to give the illusion of an encampment. The Royalist troops were, understandably, overjoyed, but the joy was short-lived, nine barrels of captured gunpowder exploding at the wall, with many men being killed and many more injured, including Hopton, who was nearly blinded.

A fortnight later the Royalists finally took Bath and, fittingly, it was the Cornishmen who first entered the city.

The monument is all that survives as a memorial to that bloody day. It was erected by Granville's grandson, Lord Lansdown, and is a huge construction. It is not what could be called elegant, but one of the inscriptions it carries is poetic, including the line 'a brighter courage and a greater disposition were never married together to make a more cheerful and innocent conversation'.

From the monument, go W down to the road, and then go up the road leading to the Royal Observer Corps Warning and Monitoring Station. Take a path skirting it to the R (N) and continue towards the trig point on top of Hangingstone Hill. The Way does not actually visit the trig point but goes L (SE) along a path that leads to yet another golf course. At this point the Way is in Somerset, having entered it from Gloucestershire during the last mile or two. The golf course is skirted by keeping to the L wall, which is followed to the far right-hand corner.

Follow Pipley Wood down and then go into open country where the Way is well marked to Little Down Hill Fort. This is the last of the hill forts on the route. Cast an eye over its well-defined single ditch and rampart and then walk across the cultivated enclosure and head for the starting gates of Bath racecourse. Beyond them is Prospect Stile, from which there is a fine view of the distinctive Kelston Round Hill, with its wooded summit.

The Way drops down from Prospect Stile and follows an obvious

The memorial to Sir Bevil Granville on Lansdown

track that skirts Kelston Round Hill to the E. It should be noted
that the inviting detour to the summit is not on a right of way. Go
down to Pendean Farm where the route leaves the lane as it swings
L (E) to go over Penn Hill, the last hill. From here the view of Bath
is expansive. A few yards from the trig point on top of the hill is a
break in the hedge L (NE) and from there the walker goes down and
into the village of Weston.

Weston is now decisively linked to Bath, but it was not always so,
and as a village it had a claim to fame as the birthplace of St
Alphege, whose day was one of the chief dates of the Saxon
calendar. He was a churchman of considerable reputation in the late
10c, having first been a monk at the Benedictine monastery of
Deerhurst, then later, in 994, Bishop of Winchester and, in 1006,
Archbishop of Canterbury. When the Danes took Canterbury, they
took Alphege, holding him prisoner, possibly as a hostage or for
ransom. Eventually his usefulness ran out and he was taken to
Greenwich where he was stoned to death.

The church stands overlooking what was the old village and is
reached by steps from the High Street. It was rebuilt in 1831, though
the tower is older and it stands on a site that is Norman at least, and
possibly Saxon. It is a pleasant church with good carvings in stone
and wood, whose chief interest lies in its memorial tablets of which
there are many, some with long inscriptions. The patient seeker will
find one to Dr William Oliver, the author of several books on
medicine and inventor of the Bath Oliver biscuit, who died in 1764.

Here also lies Samuel Purlewent, whose family name is
commemorated in the road name a little way from the church, and
on the suggested route. He was a remarkable person, an attorney of
great eminence practising from Lincoln's Inn, and a freeman of
Bath, whose will was as remarkable a feature as any in his life. In it he
stipulated that he should be buried at Weston without any parade or
coach and with no relations present. His body was to be carried by
six poor men of Weston and the congregation was to consist of six
poor men and six poor women also of the village. He was to be
buried at noon, and for their services the poor were to receive half a
guinea, and a meal consisting of boiled ham, a dozen fowls, a sirloin
of beef and plum puddings. Five guineas were set aside for the food

Kelston Round Hill from Prospect Stile, Lansdown (top) and the route to Weston from Penn Hill (below)

and they were directed to be merry and cheerful, 'for I conceive it a mere farce to put on the grimace of weeping, crying, snivelling and the like, which can answer no good end, either to the living or dead, and which I reprobate in the highest terms'.

To ensure the merry cheerfulness, Purlewent added a codicil requesting that, after he was buried, a local public-house should be supplied with another sirloin of beef, potatoes, a fillet of veal and plenty of good ale. He hoped that there 'they will refresh themselves with decency and propriety'.

From the church go via Church Road to Purlewent Drive, going R into it and following it to a small cul-de-sac on the L (N) side. Here take the footpath to the foot of Primrose Hill from where steps lead to Summerhill Road. The Way then continues easily via Sion Hill and the path across the golf course to enter Bath proper through the Royal Victoria Park.

John Wood, a local historian, wrote a history of Bath in 1765 and in it recounted as fact the following story on the origin of the city.

In 744 BC Brutus, with a group of fellow Trojans, landed at Totnes in Devon. After defeating the local people, a race of giants, they established a kingdom that extended from the Tamar to the Wiltshire-Gloucestershire borders. The royal line from Brutus reached, by the seventh generation, King Hudibras, who had a son, Bladud. Unfortunately Bladud contracted leprosy and the court, understandably anxious to avoid contamination, banished him. Bladud travelled to Keynsham where he took a job as a swineherd. In time the pigs contracted leprosy and, in an effort to avoid this being detected, Bladud took his herd to Swineswick (Swainswick). Near his hiding-place was a spot where the pigs, while rooting for acorns amongst the trees, occasionally found mud to wallow in, and Bladud noticed that one pig, which he lost for about a week, had been cured of the leprosy. Bladud tried the mud cure on himself; after a week he, too, was cured of the disease, and returned to his father's palace. In 505 BC Bladud travelled to Athens, where he was given the name 'Abaris the Sage' and taught Zoroaster magic and Pythagoras philosophy. In 483 BC he returned to England to succeed his father and, once settled, he built a capital – Caer Badon, the City of Bath, or Aquae Sulis (Waters of the Sun). Finally he reached the limit of his knowledge, and the end of his life, when a pair of wings he had invented failed to live up to his expectations on their proving-flight from the top of the Temple of Apollo. He was succeeded, in 463 BC, by Shakespeare's King Lear. Bath has, currently, two statues to Bladud, at King's and Cross Baths. The one at King's was erected in 1699, and commemorates him as 'son of Hudibras, eighth king of the Britons, a great philosopher and mathematician bred at Athens and first discoverer and founder of these baths 863 BC and 2,562 years to the present year 1699'.

The truth is rather more prosaic. Doubtless the earliest men were aware of the hot springs which gush forth every day, with little variation, a quarter of a million gallons of water at 50°C (120°F), but the first real interest in them was shown by the Romans. Following

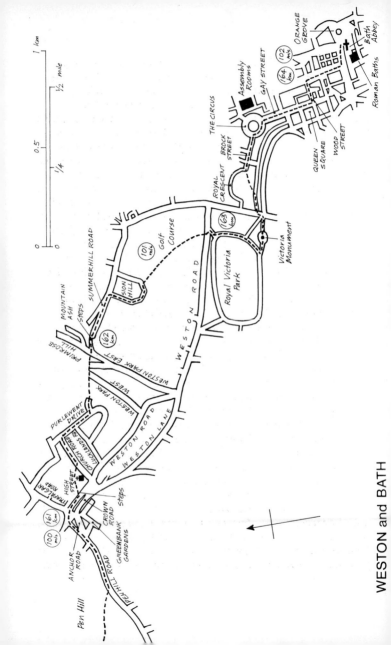

WESTON and BATH

the invasion of AD 43 the Romans swept westwards, capturing, one after the other, the hill forts of the defeated natives, including the most magnificent one at Maiden Castle. The Romans quickly established a frontier zone stretching along a line from Exeter through Gloucester and Leicester to the Humber and soon pushed a road through it, the Fosse Way. This road passed close to the place in the middle of a swamp where hot water came gushing out, and the Romans, with their history of exploiting such places, took up the challenge. From their point of view, the site was ideal; the earth supplied the water, the Cotswolds to the north supplied a stone that was easy to work and yet hardened when exposed, and the Mendips to the south supplied lead for the piping and limestone for the mortar. The town that they built around the outflow was typically Roman, with its baths, houses and temples. The temples were dedicated to the Roman Minerva, the goddess of Wisdom, and, in accordance with Roman tradition, a local Celtic sun-god Sul. That there was a real Celtic influence in the town can be seen in the superb male Gorgon's head now displayed in the Roman Baths museum, a mixture of Roman artistry and Celtic ferocity.

The Roman town lasted for 400 years and then collapsed over a relatively short period. With the withdrawal of the Roman armies in the early years of the 5c, the province of Britain was increasingly exposed to attacks by the Saxons. The area around Bath was not itself attacked until the late 6c, but by then the process of decay was well under way in the villas and temples, many of their stones being taken by the farmers in the surrounding area to build and repair their walls. Following the battle of Dyrham in AD 577, the Saxons took the three towns of Gloucester, Cirencester and Bath (then known as Akeman or Bathanceaster). The Saxons recorded that the town itself was in ruins, but they were impressed with the high standard of the buildings, which was far in advance of anything they were capable of. They described the town as the work of giants. A Saxon poem of the 8c records the town as being a ghostly ruin, with crumbling masonry and dark pools, overgrown and left to the birds, but still impressive. It seems that, even after Dyrham, the Saxons did not settle finally in the area, but waited until 658 when the battle of Peoman, believed to have taken place near Frome, made the area

The Roman baths, Bath

totally secure. Offa founded an abbey to St Peter at Hat Batha in the early part of his reign, around 760, but it was in a place that was already sacred to the Saxons. Under the influence of Dunstan, Abbot of nearby Glastonbury, this abbey became Benedictine in the 10c and saw, in 973, the coronation of King Edgar performed by the same Dunstan, by then Archbishop of Canterbury. This was the first coronation of a King who was rightly entitled to call himself King of England, and its 1,000th anniversary was the subject of a great celebration in Bath in 1973. That the ceremony of 973 took place in Bath shows that the site was of considerable secular importance at the time, and there has been a lasting Saxon influence there. The river, however, retains the British name, 'Afon', a river.

Following the Norman Conquest, the town suffered badly in the conflict between William Rufus and his barons, being virtually destroyed. To re-establish the abbey, and therefore the town, Rufus in 1088 ordered the then Bishop of Bath and Wells to make his seat at Bath. The Bishop, Rufus's physician, John de Villula (John of Tours), did so and set about the construction of a cathedral so large that the present Abbey occupies only the site of its nave. At the same time the bishop promoted, or rediscovered, the medicinal qualities of the water and Bath began to be recognised as a healing centre. By the 12c the sick were arriving from all over the country to bathe in the waters, and the town was benefiting from the trade. At that time there were 5 baths – King's, Cross and Hot being public, with the Abbot's and the Prior's reserved for the Abbey.

For a considerable time the history of Bath is the history of the Abbey, which will be dealt with later. In addition to the Abbey, the town derived some wealth in the Middle Ages from its share of the local wool trade, a share that seems to have been small in view of the area's available resources of fuller's earth and water power. As with Winchcombe, it is probable that the Abbey contributed to the wealth of the town by the process now know as spin-off, and in addition the baths helped the general prosperity. Besides the obvious gain from an influx of visitors, there were more clandestine activities. In 1449 it was said that when the bathers 'through modesty and shame try to cover their privy parts, the men with drawers and the women with smocks, they, the said people, barbarously and shamelessly strip them of the said garments and reveal them to the gaze of the bystanders, and inflict on them not only the loss of their garments, but a heavy monetary fine'.

At this time the baths themselves were notable for their unpleasantness. All were open to the air and so filthy that they were said to stink. In 1533 the antiquary John Leland visited the Cross Bath, so called from the cross in the centre. He described it as 'much frequentid of People diseased with Lepre, Pokkes, Scabbes and great Aches'. Later in the 16c, after the dissolution of the Abbey and a reduction in the wool trade, the town corporation realised the harm such conditions could do to its most valuable asset and appointed a full-time, paid attendant. This resulted in the baths being emptied and filled weekly, and in their being closed for two hours daily at midday to allow them to purge themselves of the filth from the dirty and diseased users. The latter procedure can have had little useful result, but the general improvement, coupled with a visit from Elizabeth I in 1574 and a general extolling of the virtues of the waters by physicians, heralded a new era of prosperity in the 17c. The new era can be dated from 1613, when Anne of Denmark, the Queen of James I, visited the town to bathe. For her a new bath, Queen's, was built and named. This bath was later pulled down to reveal the Roman Baths. Queen Anne's was the first of many such royal visits, both by herself and later by Charles I and his Queen, Henrietta Maria. The upswing in prosperity slackened for a period with the outbreak of the Civil War. The town was originally garrisoned by Royalist forces, but when these departed for Wells they were replaced by Parliamentarians. Like many other Cotswold towns, Bath seemed to be interested mainly in peace and treated each force in the same way. The Parliamentarian governor was Sir William Waller, and the closest Bath came to real war was in 1643 when, as we have seen, Sir William's troops fought the Royalists at the battle of Lansdown. Following that battle, the Royalists took the town and held it until 1645, when they were called upon to surrender by a besieging Parliament force. The town had been made defensible at the outbreak of the war by the rebuilding of the walls and the installation of guns, so the surrender order was refused. The Royalists' will to fight was low, however, not surprisingly in view of the crushing defeats their cause had had inflicted upon it at Naseby and other fields and, when the Parliamentarians attacked at night and seized the S gate, the Bath garrison immediately surrendered.

Little remains of Bath from this early period of its prosperity, much having been destroyed during the extensive 18c building, but there are noteworthy exceptions. Sally Lunn's House, in North Parade, was built for the Duke of Kingston in 1480, though the frontage was constructed in the 17c around the time when the house was famous as a coffee tavern run by Sally Lunn, the pastrycook. Today it is a restaurant. Abbey Church House, behind the Cross Bath, was built in the late 16c for Sir Walter Hungerford, but occupied the site of an old leper hospital dating from the 12c. There are also some 17c houses in Broad Street.

The next upswing in Bath's fortunes was due to the visits in 1702 and 1703 of Queen Anne, which gave rise to an influx of the rich and fashionable, bringing with them their craze for gambling. The scene was set for the arrival of that most famous of Bath's citizens, Beau Nash.

Richard Nash was born in Swansea in 1674, the son of a wealthy glass-merchant father. He had an eventful early life, leaving Oxford because of a scandal involving a woman, and the Guards because they did not suit his inclinations. In 1695, at only 21, he organised a pageant for the King, William of Orange, and was accepted into high society. He arrived in Bath in 1705 a little short of funds, and won a considerable sum in a short time at the gambling tables. To regulate the social life of the town, the corporation had taken to appointing Masters of Ceremonies, and when the current one, Captain Webster, a well-known bully, was finally killed in a duel, Nash was given the job, one that he was to keep for over 50 years. Under Nash's guidance the city became the social centre of England, expanding with a rush of fine building including theatres and assembly rooms. The gambling went on apace also and became so excessive that eventually an Act of Parliament was passed in 1739 limiting it, and making illegal some specific forms. Nash was never paid as MC, receiving instead a share of house profits which he used to support an extravagant life style with fine clothes and houses, and a gilt coach with 6 horses. He died in 1761 at the great age of 87, by then supported by his friends, and embittered by having had to sell most of his possessions. At his death he was mourned for his kindness and consideration – for instance, he helped raise money for the construction of a hospital – although there were also those who had latterly seen him not as a kindly old man but as an old bore with a dubious and less than endearing past. The statue of him in the Pump Room was erected in 1752, and his last house near the Theatre Royal is now a restaurant named after his last mistress, Juliana Popjoy. She was a somewhat eccentric lady herself, who after his death left the house and went to live in a hollow tree.

The Bath of Nash seems to have been an endless round of gatherings in the Assembly Rooms, walks along the laid-down routes, theatres, dances and, of course, gambling. Nash ordered that everything should cease at 11 o'clock, and stopped the extortion practised by the sedan chairmen by introducing a single sixpenny fare to anywhere in the city and a ten-shilling fine for swearing at the passengers. But Bath could not have been the social centre it was without the buildings erected to house the fashionable visitors and residents. For these we have to thank a group of architects, chiefly the Woods, father and son, supported by the remarkable Ralph Allen. Allen was a Cornishman who had rented an ailing postal service from a grateful government for 7 years, made it highly profitable through efficient management, and in the process become a rich man. He arrived in Bath in 1710 and, seeing the potential for development, bought the Combe Down stone quarries. With this stone, and the genius of John Wood the elder, a Yorkshire architect, Bath was transformed. The tradition was carried on by Wood's son, John the younger, and a group of young architects. The Georgian architecture is in the Palladian style, named after the Italian Andrea Palladia (1518–1580), and many of the finest pieces are on our route. After Nash's death, the social system continued much as before but, as new MCs could not sustain his pace, the endless round became boring and lifeless. Eventually Bath became that most alarming of things, respectable, and promptly died as a social centre. With its death some of the grandiose building schemes died as well, but sufficient had been completed to make Bath a museum of 18c architecture.

The bubble burst around 1800 and Bath changed character yet again, becoming an industrial city with a remarkable sense of its own history, particularly after the discovery of the Roman Baths.

After passing through the Royal Victoria Park, the walker reaches the Victoria monument, a large and ugly stone memorial with inscriptions on all sides commemorating different milestones in Queen Victoria's life. From the monument go, by way of an elegant gateway with sphinxes, into Royal Avenue, with its superb avenue of horse-chestnuts. L from here is Royal Crescent, perhaps the most famous of all the Bath buildings. The Crescent was the first of its kind in England and was completed in 1774 by John Wood the

Pulteney Bridge, Bath

younger. It comprises 30 houses with 114 Ionian columns and
enjoyed, at its completion, an uninterrupted view S. No. 1 has been
authentically restored as a Georgian residence and is open to the
public. The Crescent has seen some famous residents – Sir Isaac
Pitman lived at No. 12 after he arrived from Wotton-under-Edge,
and Sheridan eloped with Elizabeth Linley from No. 11.

From the Crescent, go along Brock Street, another creation of
John Wood the younger, and into the Circus which was built over
more than 20 years by the Woods, father and son. It is thought to
be the supreme achievement of the elder Wood, and comprises three
sections each of 11 houses with 648 Doric, Ionian and Corinthian
columns in three tiers surmounted by a parapet with an acorn motif
in deference to the legendary founder. William Pitt, MP for Bath and
Prime Minister, lived in a house that is now Nos. 7 and 8,
Gainsborough lived at No. 17 and in the 19c the explorer David
Livingstone lived at No. 13.

From the Circus go S down Gay Street. This was also the
combined work of the Woods, and the younger Wood lived at
No. 41. Josiah Wedgwood, whose pottery is famous, lived in No. 30.
Gay Street ends at Queen Square, another principal work of Wood
the elder, who lived at No. 24. Dr Oliver, the inventor of the Bath
Oliver, buried at Weston, also lived here. The plain obelisk in the
square was erected by Beau Nash in honour of Frederick, Prince of
Wales.

Bath contains much that is of interest that is not on our route
through the town. There is the Museum of Costume, near the
Circus; the Carriage Museum, behind the Circus; the Toy Museum,
in Milsom Street; the Victoria Art Gallery, Bridge Street; the
Geology Museum, Queen Square; the American Museum,
Claverton Down; and the Museum of Bookbinding, Manvers Street.
But for the moment meander slowly through the narrow streets to
the Roman Baths, and the Abbey. The Baths themselves are worthy
of a visit to see the museum housing the finest excavated pieces from
the Roman era, including the famous Gorgon's head, and to marvel
at the central heating system and sophisticated construction of the
great Bath itself. But even from within the Bath the eye is drawn
frequently to the Abbey which overshadows it.

The Abbey as we see it is the result of the dream of Oliver King, Bishop in the late 15c. Work was started around 1499, the Abbey being considerably smaller than the Norman Cathedral it replaced. Not all the Abbey is new; note, for instance, the end wall of the Norman chapel where the window is contained within an arch of the original Cathedral.

To attempt to convey the beauty and majesty of the Abbey in a few words is a hopeless task, but the visitor should look out at least for the following outstanding features.

The largest monument is to James Montague, Bishop of Bath and Wells from 1608 until 1615, when he became Bishop of Winchester. It is an imposing work, as are the superb fan-vaulted ceilings of the nave and aisles. That of the N aisle contains rows of painted heraldic shields. The E window contains 817 sq. ft of glass and was restored following war damage. The outstanding piece of stonework is the chantry chapel of William Birde standing on the S side of the chancel. The work was so intricate and, therefore, so expensive that it is said to have bankrupted Birde. The chancel also contains statues of St Alphege, St Dunstan, and Bishops John de Villula and Oliver King. In the S transept is the tomb of Sir William Waller's wife.

This list cannot be exhaustive, but since it is fitting to regard the Abbey as the end of the Cotswold Way, the walker can relax here and spend some time exploring. The exploration, like the Way itself, will be rewarding.

The rocks underlying the route are sedimentary, having been laid down during the Jurassic period of the Mesozoic era. This era began about 225 million years ago with the Triassic period. The Jurassic followed this, the era coming to a close with the Cretaceous period.

The Mesozoic era represents the transition from the relatively primitive animals and plants of the Paleozoic era to the more modern forms of the Cainozoic, that began 63 million years ago. The rocks of the Cotswolds were laid down while dinosaurs lived on the land, and ammonites, the best known of the fossils found today, were abundant. The first mammals, flowering plants and birds were also just appearing.

Jurassic limestones form the Cotswold escarpment from Chipping Campden to Bath, while the broad Severn Vale that it overlooks is formed of the mostly softer Jurassic Lias clays and sands. The N and mid-Cotswold scarp is formed of Inferior Oolitic limestone and it is here that the range attains its maximum height of 1,070 ft at Cleeve Hill. To the S, and, in general, to the E, the Great Oolitic limestone of the hills overlooking the Avon valley near Bath gradually overlays the Inferior Oolite and the general height of the range falls to around 600 to 750 ft.

Nearly all the rivers to the W of the Cotswold scarp flow into the Severn, while those to the E follow the dip-slope, gently falling away towards the Oxford Clay Vales, to join the Thames. The Avon is an exception to this drainage pattern, apparently superimposed on the present rocks after the regular Mesozoic rocks, on which its course began, had been worn away. It rises NE of Bristol and flows E for 10 miles, then SW and W and finally N through Bath.

At several places the Cotswold escarpment has been eroded back to leave behind remnants of the former scarp, in the shape of 'outliers'. Examples are Churchdown, Robin's Wood and Bredon Hills, which can be seen from the various viewpoints on the more northerly stretches of the Way.

Towards the end of the Triassic period, seas intermittently covered the area, causing the deposition of marine strata. By the early Jurassic period there was consistent sea-covering under which the purely marine Liassic rocks were laid down, followed by the limestones. Thus we have, simplified, a typical Jurassic succession of clays, forming the low-lying plains; sandy rocks, forming the foothills; and limestones, forming the hills. The clays suggest a deep, muddy sea containing ammonites and marine reptiles, while the sands suggest a shallower sea and the limestone a clear sea with corals, sea lilies and associated animals.

The Lower Liassic clays were laid down about 170 to 180 million years ago and gradually decrease in thickness from 960 ft in the Vale of Evesham to about 200 ft around Bristol. The Middle Lias are topped by a marlstone rock bed that is hard in relation to the soft sands and clays above and below, and has produced a platform or ledge below the scarp. The Upper Liassic rocks lie, in the mid-Cotswolds, in a succession from a thin layer of Upper Lias clay, through about 200 ft of yellow Cotteswold sand to the 20 ft-thick Cephalopod beds, a ferruginous oolitic limestone containing abundant fossils, and the Scissum beds, a sandy limestone. S towards Bath the Cephalopod beds pass into the Cotswold sands while to the N both of these pass into the Upper Lias clay which thickens to about 200 ft at Cleeve Hill.

The formation of the inferior limestone was interrupted by earth movements causing warping of the sea floor, as is well shown by the structures in the Cheltenham area. Here the warp formed a basin into which the Lower Inferior Oolitic was deposited. There followed the formation of a synclinal fold around Cleeve Hill as well as a general uplift. Deposition occurred in the basin while erosion occurred elsewhere until the whole area was submerged and the laying down of the Middle Inferior Oolite began. At the end of this period, widespread folding took place, and the Painswick and Cleeve Hill synclines were finally shaped. In addition the Birdlip anticline was formed. The whole Cotswold area was then elevated, eroded and then once more submerged for the Upper Inferior Oolite to be laid down.

The Great Oolitic series starts with the fuller's earth clay, which is between 100 and 150 ft thick in the Bath area. Stonesfield slate overlies this in the north and mid-Cotswolds and the Great Oolitic limestone, a hard, white, shelly rock, tops this in the N forming the plateau and the scarp southwards towards Bath where the famous Bath Stone is part of this series.

At Chipping Campden, where the route starts, a great variety of types of building is found, with examples of typical Cotswold tiled roofs, in an excellent state of preservation. Stonesfield slate, the traditional tiling material, is not a true slate but a fissile, sandy limestone. Its earliest known use is in the false-entrance walling of the Belas Knap long barrow. The slates, dug out easily near the surface, were known as 'presents' but, if this supply failed and they had to be mined, they were known as 'pendle'. The latter were brought to the surface in the form of large blocks which were kept in their wet state by earthing over. When the first winter frost came, the villagers would uncover the blocks and water them so that the frost would split them. The industry had its own nomenclature: a 'slatter' made the slates after a 'getter' had got them. The slates were named according to the size they were cut to. The smaller top slates were called Cocks or Tants, followed by Muffity or Becks, Bachelors, Long 16s, and finally the huge tiles at the bottom of the roofs called Cussems. The roofs were very heavy and required huge oak beams to support them; the cost of such beams helped to bring about the decline of the industry. One of the quarrying areas that can still be visited is at Sevenhampton, just off the SE edge of Cleeve Common.

The Cotswold stone-building industry has also declined greatly, other materials being more economic and, of the large number of quarries that can be seen in the area, only a few are still worked. The best of these is Coscombe, near Stumps Cross, where blocks are still obtained from the regular bedding planes of yellow Guiting stone. This Lower Inferior Oolitic rock becomes the Pea Grit southwards, as at Leckhampton.

Cleeve Hill, the highest point on the escarpment, has perhaps the most spectacular scenery, with isolated upland valleys and magnificent views. Here the Inferior Oolitic limestone is at its thickest. A walk along the old quarries at the base of the cliffs, towards Huddlestone's Table, shows the massive lower Freestone and Pea Grit beds. A couple of miles after Cleeve, the Way passes through 'Happy Valley', a dry valley without a stream. Such valleys are in evidence all over the Cotswolds. There are several theories on the formation of dry valleys, one of which suggests that they were eroded by running water in times when the rainfall and water-table, the level of underground water, were much higher, and the major scarp recession was taking place. Another suggests that they were formed at the end of the Ice Age, when the frozen limestone was impermeable.

Springs are another characteristic of the area. They may occur where valleys reach the water-table or, as is common, where a layer of clay or non-porous rock occurs. Thus many farms and settlements were placed at the junction with the Upper Lias clay, to be near the water source. In the Great Oolitic regions, the junction with the fuller's earth clay forms the springline, as seen over much of the plateau of the dip-slope.

Further on down the route, the Way reaches Leckhampton Hill, where is found the best of the now deserted Cotswold quarries. These were a source of the well-known Cheltenham building stone, and show the succession from the Lower Lias clay in the valley, past the marlstone shelf of the Middle Lias, over the slopes of the sandy Upper Lias to the cliffs that range from the pea grit through the freestones to the ragstones where the hill reaches 965 ft at its highest point.

The pea grit is a pisolithic limestone, containing 'egg-shaped' bodies about the size of a pea that are similar to, but larger than, those of the oolitic limestone above. The freestone exhibits regular spacing of the horizontal bedding planes, and of the joints at right-angles to them. These planes were brought about by a pause in the deposition process, while a change in the currents during the deposition caused 'current' bedding and a rock that builders avoided since it would develop a ragged appearance after weathering. The freestone was used by builders because of the ease of its removal in large slabs and the lack of large fossils, which gave it a fine texture enabling it to be sawn into blocks. The right-angled joints were mainly the result of tensions set up in the rock as it dried out after deposition, their regular occurrence being the result of its homogeneous nature. Above the freestones, the bedding planes are closer together and the rock is rich in fossils and has broken up irregularly. These are the ragstones that occur just below the surface over most of the N and mid-Cotswolds. Since they provide such conveniently sized stones, they have been used extensively for the dry-stone walling that is such a characteristic feature of the area. While at Leckhampton, one cannot fail to notice the famous landmark of the Devil's Chimney, which is probably nothing more than rock which was left untouched as unsuitable for building. It contains a major fissure that will play a large part in bringing about its collapse in the next 50 years. The disintegration of the rocks along its joints is due to frost erosion.

The cliffs on the W side of Crickley Hill form the finest pea grit formation in Britain. At one point along the beds a farmer has made a pillar to support the corner of a cave that has been formed in it, and at the point of the hill is the erosion-formed Devil's Table. Barrow Wake also affords a magnificent view but unfortunately the nearness of the main road has helped it to become popular, as the litter shows. The view provides an outstanding panorama over the Severn Vale to the Welsh Hills, the Malverns and beyond. The Peak, another viewpoint nearby, looks out across the Vale of Witcombe, one of the more splendid combes along the route.

There are also extensive views from the summits in the Painswick area which again is rich in deep valleys and beautiful combes. Platform terraces, formed by the marlstone rock bed, stretch up the valleys here, producing sites for farms. The deep valleys with small streams again show evidence of the falling water-table, the town itself being on a ridge between two such valleys. Painswick Hill and Haresfield Beacon are the most notable summits, and below the trig point of the Beacon there is a spectacular exposure where the junction of the Inferior Oolitic and Upper Lias sands occurs.

It is at Bath that perhaps the most attractive example is to be found of the influence of geology on Cotswold building. Here Bath stone has been used for centuries as the main building material, and it seems, going down into Bath from the hills to the N, that the whole town has been made of it. The famous Roman Baths were built of this stone, and it is still being used today; the magnificent crescents of the 18c are also constructed of it. The Roman Baths occur where the Avon crosses the Bath axis, similar to, but more prominent than, the axes of the N Cotswolds. The weaknesses in the rock here allow water to reach great depths and so become heated. Because the water can also rise rapidly to the surface, it emerges as the hot springs, with a temperature of 120°F.

Note: **NT** denotes National Trust
property